Answers

to Your
B I B L E
Questions

75 Reasons to Believe Scripture's
Truth and Trustworthiness

ED STRAUSS

BARBOUR
PUBLISHING

Published by Barbour Publishing, Inc., P.O. Box 719, Uhrichsville, Ohio 44683 www.barbourbooks.com

Our mission is to publish and distribute inspirational products offering exceptional value and biblical encouragement to the masses.

Printed in the United States of America.

Contents

1

Does the Bible as it was originally recorded contain any mistakes? Are our copies still completely error-free today?

In answer to the first question: No, the Word of God, as originally given, contains no mistakes. Paul tells us, "All Scripture is given by inspiration of God" (2 Timothy 3:16 NKJV), and God doesn't make mistakes. However, Bible scholars recognize that as the scriptures were hand-copied over the centuries, minor scribal errors crept into the text. The Bible as we have it today, therefore, is not completely free of *human* error. This is what evangelical Christians mean when they say the Bible is "inerrant in its original autographs."

While the Hebrew scribes took great care to copy the scriptures accurately, they occasionally made mistakes. This was understandable, given that the Hebrew text had no separations between words and that the words consisted of only consonants—no vowels.

During the AD 600s to 900s, Jewish scribes called Masoretes followed very strict rules for making copies of the text and added helpful vowel points to the consonants. This reduced scribal errors dramatically. The Masoretic Text (MT) was so renowned for being error-free that it was accepted as the official version of the Old Testament.

But what about inaccuracies introduced into the text *before* the Masoretes? Until 1947, skeptics argued that there were probably so many mistakes in the Hebrew text that there was no way of telling *how* closely the MT resembled the original documents.

That year, however, a remarkable discovery was made. Jars full of ancient scrolls were discovered in caves near the Dead Sea in Israel. These scrolls dated back two thousand years to between 225 BC–AD 70. The jars contained at least fragments of every Old Testament book but Esther. The "Dead Sea Scrolls," as they came to be known, have confirmed the remarkable accuracy of the Masoretic Text. Yes, there are differences between the MT and certain manuscripts, but the MT is virtually identical to a majority of the ancient copies.

2

What kinds of errors did the scribes make as they copied the text?

෩

The books of 1 and 2 Kings and their "companion" books, 1 and 2 Chronicles, include an example of what is clearly a copyist's error.

First and 2 Kings, which scholars generally agree were compiled between 562–538 BC, detail the history of the kingdoms of Israel and Judah. The parallel histories recorded in 1 and 2 Chronicles focus on Judah, and scholars date them to Ezra's day, some hundred years later. When recounting the same historical events, Chronicles usually differs from Kings only in that it supplies extra information about the kingdom of Judah.

But here's one striking discrepancy:

The writer of Kings writes, "Jehoiachin was eighteen years old when he became king, and he reigned in Jerusalem three months" (2 Kings 24:8 NKJV). However, Chronicles states: "Jehoiachin was eight years old when he became king, and he reigned in Jerusalem three months and ten days" (2 Chronicles 36:9 NKJV). The ten days is accounted for by the fact that the compiler of Chronicles is, as usual, supplying extra details. The real question is this: Was Jehoiachin eighteen or eight when he became king?

Second Kings 24:15 tells us that Jehoiachin was married at the time he became king and had more than one wife, so obviously he was eighteen, not eight. Indeed, one ancient Hebrew manuscript differs from the Masoretic Text and has "eighteen" in *both* 2 Chronicles 36:9 and 2 Kings 24:8.

So how did this error happen? Well, the Hebrew text of 2 Kings 24:8 literally reads *"son of eight ten years Jehoiachin,"* and the text for 2 Chronicles 36:9 would have originally said the same thing. Very likely, a later scribe, while copying the passage in 2 Chronicles, lost his place and his eyes skipped over the word *ten* to the next word, "years."

3

Wasn't the book of Genesis passed down as oral traditions for hundreds of years?

Skeptics have insisted that the accounts of Abraham, Isaac, and Jacob existed for hundreds of years after their day as oral traditions. That, they say, is because writing was not prevalent at that time in human history. Therefore, the argument goes, the stories—because they were passed down by word of mouth—were corrupted to such an extent that they have little or no actual historical value.

However, Genesis 11:27–28 says that Abraham (around 2166–1991 BC) emigrated from Ur in Chaldea, where writing (even schools) existed. Abraham was a shepherd by choice, but he was not an illiterate nomad. On the contrary, he was a wealthy and, very probably, literate man. In addition, thousands of clay tablets containing writing in a phonetic Semitic version of cuneiform (a writing system used in ancient times) have been discovered at the ancient city of Ebla, just two hundred miles north of Canaan. Many of these writings date to 2500 BC, hundreds of years before Abraham's birth.

In addition, the book of Genesis gives indications of being written in stages, as each succeeding generation, in their old age, added its own story to the ongoing narrative. One example of this is found in Genesis 35:27–29, which describes Jacob returning to his father in Hebron and Isaac's death a few years after. The story of Jacob's adventures in Haran was likely written then. Just *before* Isaac died, however, Jacob's son Joseph had been presumed dead. But after Jacob learned that Joseph was still alive, their combined story continues (in the period *before* Isaac's death), beginning with the statement, "This is the history of Jacob" (Genesis 37:2 NKJV).

Moreover, the cultural elements mentioned in Genesis, from traditions to laws to styles of covenants, all bear the earmarks of authenticity for the time and area in which they were said to have happened. In other words, they are accurate historical accounts.

4

How does the excavation of ancient Ebla shed light on the Bible?

In 1974–75, Italian archaeologist Paolo Matthiae was excavating the mound of Tell Mardikh in Syria when his team discovered a room containing nearly eighteen hundred clay tablets. The tablets dated from around 2500 BC to 2250 BC, the date the city was destroyed. It turns out Matthiae had unearthed the records for Ebla, an ancient city and trade empire that flourished and was sacked nearly ten centuries before Moses.

The writing on many of the tablets was in a hitherto unknown language, but as Dr. Pettinato (the team's epigrapher) deciphered them, he discovered that Ebla had a complex code of laws, many of which resembled the Old Testament commandments, which would be written about a thousand years later. Sacrifices for sin, purification rites, and even scapegoats were known in Ebla. This contradicted skeptics who had previously argued that Moses couldn't have written his law at the time of the Exodus "because codified laws didn't exist that early."

The Ebla tablets also contain many Semitic names, such as Adam, Abraham, Esau, Ishmael, David, and Saul. They also discuss the Canaanites and the Hittites and refer to ancient Urusalima (Jerusalem), Hazor, Megiddo, and other cities mentioned in the Bible.

Dr. Pettinato reported that Sodom and Gomorrah were named as cities with which Ebla traded. Other scholars dispute this, claiming that the inscriptions instead stand for the names of cities in Syria.

Much of the early speculation that the tablets contained the name of *Yah* (short for *Yahweh*) as endings of people's names is now also disputed. Nevertheless, the discovery of the ancient library of Ebla has done much to confirm many of the Bible's accounts and to shed light on the ancient civilizations that were the backdrop of the Old Testament.

5

Did ancient patriarchs like Methuselah actually live hundreds of years?

&

Until just a few years ago, many people responded with incredulity when they read the biblical accounts of the ancient patriarchs living for centuries. (Some still do.) For example, according to the scriptures, Methuselah died when he was 969 years old (Genesis 5:27).

In recent years, however, microbiologists and molecular geneticists have learned that aging is largely caused by accumulative damage to our DNA, the hereditary material found in nearly every cell in the human body. Scientists are also exploring molecular repair and rejuvenation of deteriorated cells and tissues to extend the human lifespan. They're confident that they'll eventually be able to stop the aging process so that humans will live hundreds or even thousands of years.

Suddenly, biblical patriarchs living for several centuries doesn't seem so incredible.

Many Christians believe that before the Flood

(Genesis 6–8), mankind's DNA wasn't as easily damaged or susceptible to aging as it is today. In addition, the earth's magnetic field was stronger and a layer of water (in the form of ice crystals) shielded it from most ultraviolet radiation. But after the Flood, the shielding was gone, damage to the DNA began to accumulate, and lifespans began to shorten. Shem lived 600 years, Arphaxad 438 years, Peleg 239 years, Terah 205 years, Abraham 175 years, Jacob 147 years, and Joseph 110 years (see Genesis 11:10–26, 32; 25:7; 47:28; 50:26).

Some Christians, however, believe that these great ages are not to be taken literally, but that they merely echo Babylonian myths that included accounts of ancients living many centuries. They point out that the 110 years Joseph is said to have lived was considered the "ideal age" in Egyptian society. They believe, therefore, that these numbers are symbolic.

Nevertheless, the ages of Abraham and Isaac and Jacob are so embedded in the details of their stories, and make such precise sense mathematically, that it's difficult to believe they're merely symbolic.

6

How do the patriarchs' ages make such precise sense mathematically?

&

If you compare dates within the lives of Isaac, Ishmael, Jacob, and Joseph (scattered throughout the book of Genesis), you'll see that these so-called random dates are perfectly synchronized.

Let's have a look: the Bible tells us that Isaac was sixty years old when Jacob was born (Genesis 25:26). Now, Isaac died at 180, so Jacob was 120 when his father passed away (Genesis 35:28–29). This was ten years before Jacob entered Egypt at age 130 (Genesis 47:9). This was also the second year of the famine, so Joseph was thirty-nine, since 30 + 7 good years + 2 bad years = 39 total years (Genesis 41:46, 53; 45:6).

Now, 130 – 39 = 91, so Jacob was 91 years old when Joseph was born at the end of Jacob's fourteen-year work contract with Laban (Genesis 30:25; 31:41). Since 91 – 14 = 77, Jacob was 77 (and Isaac, therefore, 137) when Isaac thought he was dying and blessed Jacob, who then fled to Haran.

Isaac believed he was about to die when he was 137, but he needn't have worried. After all, he lived another forty-three years and died at the ripe old age of 180 (Genesis 35:28). So why did he believe he was doomed to die at that age? He was fatalistic. Isaac's older brother Ishmael had died at exactly the age of 137 (Genesis 25:17), and Isaac thought *he'd* also die at that age.

Either the author of Genesis carefully worked out how all these scattered dates intricately interlocked before he begin to write, or (more likely) these are the *actual* dates that work out with such precision because they are real.

This then means that Isaac actually lived 180 years, Ishmael lived 137 years, Jacob lived 147 years, and Joseph lived 110 years—even though most of these ages are well beyond the maximum lifespan today.

7

Why does the Bible say that Philistines lived in Canaan in Abraham's day?

❧

In 1175 BC, during the reign of Ramesses III, a massive migration of people from Greece, Crete, and Anatolia launched an attack on Egypt. These invaders, whom historians call Sea Peoples, attacked Egypt by sea and by land. After being repulsed, however, they retreated and settled along the coast of Canaan. Chief among them were the Peleset (P'listi), which is why all these people groups were collectively known as *Philistines*.

However, according to the Bible, Philistines were *already* living on the coast of Canaan around 2066 BC. After Abraham made a covenant with them in Beersheba, "they returned into the land of the Philistines" and "Abraham sojourned in the Philistines' land many days" (Genesis 21:32, 34 KJV). In addition, around 1966 BC, "Isaac went unto Abimelech king of the Philistines unto Gerar" (Genesis 26:1 KJV). Also, the Philistines were said to live on the coast of Canaan around 1446 BC: "Now when Pharaoh had let the people go, God did not lead them by the way of the land of the Philistines" (Exodus 13:17 NASB).

Bible scholars believe that a later Hebrew editor designated earlier peoples as "Philistine" in the Genesis accounts; Philistines lived there in *his* day, so he called that area "the land of the Philistines" to clarify which region the text referred to.

But there's more: The lands and islands of the seafaring Sea Peoples were *near* Canaan and had already traded with the Canaanites for centuries. No doubt, many had immigrated and settled peacefully among the Canaanites along the coast, especially at Gerar. Since they came from the same lands as the *later* ethnic groups called Philistines, the Bible editor referred to these earlier Sea Peoples as Philistines also—since they *were*.

8

Why would Abimelech fall for the "she's-my-sister" deception twice?

Abraham herded sheep and goats in the Negev, the wilderness south of Canaan. He had to move north during dry years to find pasture and grain supplies in cities there. This brought a new danger: Abraham's wife Sarah was so beautiful that he was afraid someone might kill him to take her. So when strangers asked who she was, he'd say she was his sister (Genesis 12:10–20; 20:12–13). In around 2066 BC, Abraham moved to Gerar, where he told the king Abimelech that Sarah was his sister (Genesis 20:1–15).

Circa 1966 BC, after Abraham's death, his son Isaac used the same stratagem for the same reason. "Isaac went unto Abimelech king of the Philistines unto Gerar. . . . And the men of the place asked him of his wife; and he said, She is my sister" (Genesis 26:1, 7 KJV). Abimelech only discovered Isaac's deception after "a long time" (Genesis 26:8–11).

In both cases, the deception was not only wrong, but unnecessary. But the question many ask is: How can we believe Abimelech would have been dumb enough to fall for the same trick *twice*? Those who believe that the Bible wasn't inspired by God but is merely the product of human authors say that *one* event was carelessly duplicated.

The answer is much more straightforward and simple: The Abimelech who was king of Gerar in Isaac's day was *not* the same Abimelech who had been king in Abraham's day. This was, after all, a hundred years later. He was most likely Abimelech's grandson who had been named after him. Isaac had probably heard his father and mother talk of their ruse, so when he found himself in a similar situation a century later, he decided to try it as well.

9

Were the plagues of Egypt outright miracles, or are there natural explanations?

৶৹

Scholars have noted that nine of the ten plagues of Exodus were events that naturally occurred in Egypt from late summer to spring. This may be one reason Pharaoh refused to believe they were divine acts. However, other Egyptians *were* convinced that the God of the Hebrews was judging their homeland (Exodus 8:19; 9:20).

Here are the first nine plagues and how they fit in with what often occurred naturally in Egypt:

(1) Plague of blood (7:14–24): the Nile flooded in late summer; heavy rains in the red-soil region of Lake Victoria could have choked the river with blood-red silt.

(2) Plague of frogs (8:1–14): when the fish died (7:21), the frogs fled to land and died.

(3) Plague of gnats (8:16–19): gnats bred in the flooded fields of Egypt in late fall. With no frogs to

keep them in check, they (and flies) reproduced in record numbers.

(4) Plague of flies (8:20–32): as the Nile receded, flies began to breed and "dense swarms of flies poured. . .throughout Egypt" (Exodus 8:24 NIV).

(5) Plague on livestock (9:1–7): this may have been a disease carried by biting flies.

(6) Plague of boils (9:8–12): likely also an epidemic transmitted by flies.

(7) Plague of hail (9:13–35): hailstorms happened in January and February.

(8) Plague of locusts (10:1–20): east winds often swept in locusts in March and April.

(9) Plague of darkness (10:21–23): likely caused by a severe *khamsin*, a sandstorm (darkness that could be "felt"—verse 21) that normally occurred every March or April.

These may have been "natural events," but they were miraculously amplified. For example, hailstorms happened, but as God warned, "I will send the worst hailstorm that has ever fallen on Egypt, from the day it was founded till now" (Exodus 9:18 NIV).

And then there's the plague on the firstborn (12:29–30). This selective judgment was clearly an unnatural miracle. After this final plague in April, Pharaoh finally allowed the Hebrews to leave Egypt.

10

Can the Red Sea parting be explained as God using natural phenomena to accomplish divine purposes?

&

We often think that for something to be a miracle, it must defy all known laws of nature. Thus, when we read in Exodus 14:21–22 of God parting the Red Sea and creating walls of water on the right and left hand, we envision water rising vertically, defying gravity. And this is possible for God. After all, He *created* the world and the laws of physics that govern matter.

Moses said, "The floods stood upright like a heap; the depths congealed in the heart of the sea" (Exodus 15:8 NKJV). The word *congealed* means "hardened." That doesn't mean the Red Sea was frozen but that something strange happened to the water. The normal laws of nature were bending to the miracle-working power of God.

God could also have amplified *existing* laws of nature to bring about His desired result. For example, although English Bibles read "Red Sea," the Hebrew words *yam suph* mean "Sea of Reeds"—which seems to refer to a body of water that is shallower yet deep enough to drown in. Thus, many scholars believe that the Hebrews crossed the sea at the present-day Bitter Lakes, just north of the Red Sea.

Another detail to bear in mind: "The Lord caused the sea to go back by a strong east wind all that night, and made the sea dry land, and the waters were divided" (Exodus 14:21 KJV). This "strong east wind" is specifically named as *the* cause. Even today, a phenomena called "wind setdown" (sustained east-west winds) at the Bitter Lakes pushes the waters aside and exposes the lake bottom, allowing Arabs to cross. In Moses' day, God could have stopped the wind abruptly, causing the water to rush back with punishing force upon Pharaoh's chariot army.

No matter *how* God did the miracle, He did it—and the Hebrews escaped Egypt.

11

Do any ancient Egyptian records mention the events of the Exodus?

At least one may do so. A papyrus called the *Admonitions of Ipuwer* describes the land of Egypt in chaos, the Nile turning to blood, and slaves plundering their masters. It also describes the breakdown of law and order, as well as famine following natural catastrophes. It is exactly the situation one would expect to see in Egypt in the months after devastating plagues, widespread destruction of trees and crops, and the wiping out of Egypt's army.

Scholars agree that this papyrus was written no later than the Nineteenth Dynasty. That's the time of Ramesses II, so it could refer to events after an Exodus in 1250 BC. However, most scholars agree that this is a copy of an *earlier* scroll—so it more likely refers to an Exodus in 1446 BC.

Exodus 7:20, 24 (NIV) says: "He raised his staff. . . and struck the water of the Nile, and all the water was changed into blood. . . . And all the Egyptians dug along the Nile to get drinking water." Meanwhile, Ipuwer 2.10 says: "Indeed, the river is blood, yet men drink of it. Men. . .thirst after water."

Exodus 11:2; 12:36 (NKJV) says, "let every man ask from his neighbor and every woman from her neighbor, articles of silver and articles of gold. . . . Thus they plundered the Egyptians." Ipuwer 3:3 says, "Indeed, gold and lapis lazuli, silver and turquoise, carnelian and amethyst. . .are strung on the necks of maidservants."

Apart from several parallels to the Bible, Ipuwer describes the state of his country after the power of the government was temporarily broken and anarchy reigned.

Pharaoh Amenhotep II reigned 1454–1419 BC. He conducted ambitious foreign military campaigns until the ninth year of his reign—which (counting 1454 as his first year) would have been 1446 BC, the time of the Exodus. After that, Amenhotep did no more military exploits.

12

Was the biblical Exodus from Egypt a literal event? If so, when did it take place?

The biblical story of the Exodus of the people of Israel from Egypt was a literal event. The question is, when did it happen? For centuries, biblical historians generally believed it happened around 1446 BC, because 1 Kings 6:1 states that Solomon began to build the Temple in the fourth year of his reign, which was also the 480th year after the Exodus. That was 966 BC, and 966 + 480 = 1446. This means that the invasion of Canaan began forty years after that, in 1406 BC.

In the last century, however, scholars began to favor a later date for the Exodus (around 1250 BC). There are a few reasons for this:

First, the Philistines settled Canaan's coast in 1175 BC. This fits with Shamgar fighting Philistines around 1150 BC (after an Exodus in 1250 BC). But according to an Exodus in 1446 BC, the Philistines would not *arrive* until 150 years after Shamgar. But as has already been explained, pre-Philistine Sea Peoples had already been present in Canaan for hundreds of years.

Second, Exodus 1:11 (NIV) says that the Hebrew slaves "built Pithom and Rameses as store cities for Pharaoh," which seems to indicate that Rameses II was the Pharaoh of the oppression and Exodus. Yet Genesis 47:11 says that Joseph settled his family in "the district of Rameses" four hundred-some years *before* Rameses II. Clearly, this was the home district of the powerful Rameses family.

Third, those who believe in an Exodus in 1250 BC point out that Hazor was burned around 1200 BC. That's true; however, Hazor was *also* burned around 1400 BC—yet became a center of Canaanite power again afterwards. Also, the destruction and burning of Jericho fits well with the 1400 BC date, but by 1200 BC Jericho had been in ruins for two hundred years.

Finally, an early Exodus (1446 BC) means not having to explain away the 480 years as "symbolic," and not having to cram all the Judges into nearly half the time.

13

Who actually wrote the Torah, the Books of the Law?

Moses was a real, historical person, and the Torah (the first five books of the Old Testament) repeatedly states that he wrote God's Law (See Exodus 24:3–4; Numbers 33:2; Deuteronomy 31:9, 22, 24).

However, around 1877, the German scholar Julius Wellhausen argued in the Documentary Hypothesis (also called the Wellhausen Hypothesis) that the Law was fabricated (in Moses' name) hundreds of years *after* Moses' death. This hypothesis is also called JEDP, because it states that the Law was created from four sources:

(J) The Jehovah/Yahweh source, written around 950 BC in Judah

(E) The Elohim/El source, written around 850 BC in northern Israel

(D) The Deuteronomic source, written around 600 BC in Judah

(P) The Priestly source, written around 500 BC

by priests during the Babylonian Exile

Finally, according to Wellhausen, redactors (editors) combined all the sources, creating the Torah in its present form around 450 BC.

This hypothesis was widely believed until 1987, when biblical scholar R. N. Whybray pointed out the logical fallacies of JEDP. Whybray asked why, if the Yahweh and Elohim sources scrupulously avoided duplication and contradictory themes, did the final editor (trying to create a *believable* "pious fraud") deliberately combine them? Since then, many conflicting, sometimes radically different, theories have replaced Wellhausen's hypothesis.

Not only does the Torah itself state that Moses wrote it, but other early Bible books also refer to the Law existing in *their* day. Joshua "read all the words of the law" (Joshua 8:34–35 NKJV) at the beginning of the conquest of Canaan around 1406 BC. And as he was dying around 970 BC, David told Solomon to "keep the charge of the LORD your God [*Yahweh Elohim*]: to walk in His ways, to keep His statutes, His commandments, His judgments, and His testimonies, as it is written in the Law of Moses" (1 Kings 2:3 NKJV).

14

If Moses wrote the Torah, how can we explain references to events that happened *after* his death?

❧

There is no doubt that the Torah includes accounts of events that happened after Moses' death. Conservative scholars agree, for example, that Moses didn't write Deuteronomy 34, which actually describes his death. Obviously, another inspired writer added this passage. And Moses wouldn't have written Numbers 12:3, which proclaims how humble he was. But the fact is, Moses wrote about 99 percent of the Torah.

Here's another example: the author of the book of Joshua tells us, "And the name of Hebron formerly was Kirjath Arba" (Joshua 14:15 NKJV). Yet Genesis 35:27 (NKJV) refers to "Kirjath Arba (that is, Hebron)" and Genesis 13:18 simply calls it "Hebron." Again, God had a later editor add these updates to Genesis.

When were such notes added? Well, two times in Israel's history, their entire alphabet changed, and this required transliterating the scriptures—writing them out in the new alphabets.

The Sinaitic alphabet was commonly used for writing throughout Sinai, Canaan, and Phoenicia in Moses' day, so he probably wrote the Law (in Hebrew) in *that* alphabet. But by around 1000 BC, the Israelites' alphabet had changed and they then used "paleo-Hebrew" letters. (Examples of this are the Gezer calendar, the Siloam inscription, and the Samaritan alphabet.)

The prophet Samuel was alive at that very time; he and Moses were the two godliest men in Israel's history (Jeremiah 15:1; 1 Samuel 3:19–21). The same God who inspired Moses to write the scriptures could have inspired Samuel to transliterate and annotate them.

The second time the Israelites changed their alphabet was around 500–450 BC, when the Aramaic alphabet replaced paleo-Hebrew writing. (This was when the modern, square-lettered Hebrew alphabet came into use.) Again, a wise, godly scholar was alive to transliterate the scriptures. His name was Ezra (see Ezra 7:6; Nehemiah 8:2, 8). He was the most eminent scholar in Israel's history and is believed to have written the books of Ezra and Nehemiah and to have compiled both books of Chronicles.

15

What does the Law of Moses
really say about slavery?

❧

Slavery in ancient Israel was not the same as what was practiced in the past in the United States. In America, slave traders actually *sold* men and women who then became the property of their owners. Slaves in America had no rights and couldn't appeal to a judge if their owners overworked or mistreated them. They were often organized into slave gangs and worked under degrading, intolerable conditions.

In ancient Israel, it was usually the decision of the person himself or herself to become a slave. Slaves at this time did this to relieve a situation of severe poverty or to pay off a large debt. When they were desperate for financial security, they would "sell themselves" as servants. For example, Jacob served Laban for fourteen years to pay his bride-price and marry Laban's daughters (Genesis 29:15–30).

The become-a-servant clauses in the Law were written to improve the lot of the impoverished, not to enrich the owners. Slaves had rights, and the Law warned against mistreating them (Leviticus 25:35–43; Exodus 21:20). For example, if a master struck a slave and injured his eye or knocked out a tooth, the slave became free (Exodus 21:26–27). Most slaves were domestic servants, doing the work of a normal laborer. Enterprising slaves could even do business and buy their freedom (Leviticus 25:48–49). After serving six years, Hebrew servants were to be set free, and the master was to send them out with abundant provisions (Deuteronomy 15:12–15).

Furthermore, the laws regulating servitude in Israel were more humane than in the rest of the ancient Middle East. Therefore, Moses' Law specified that if slaves from another country fled to Israel for refuge, the Israelites were not to return them to their former masters but were commanded to allow them to live "wherever they like and in whatever town they choose" (Deuteronomy 23:15–16 NIV).

16

How could Leviticus 11 be the inerrant Word of God when it contains factual misinformation about rabbits?

In Leviticus 11, God told the Israelites, "The rabbit, though it chews the cud, does not have a divided hoof; it is unclean for you" (verse 6 NIV).

However, as Bible critics point out, the rabbit—or "hare" in some translations—does *not* regurgitate its cud and chew it a second time the way cattle and other ruminants do. Though it's a minor detail, there are three such instances in this one chapter. This perplexes many Christians. And the question that comes to mind is, "If the Bible is wrong about *these* things, what *else* is it mistaken about?"

First of all, rabbits *do* chew the cud. So do capybaras, hamsters, and other related species. They just don't get it back in their mouths the way larger, hoofed ruminants do. Many rabbit owners are concerned when they see their pets eating their own feces, but the animals are, in fact, *not* eating feces but *cecotropes*—cuds of half-digested plant matter.

Rabbits have a large cecum situated between their small and large intestines, where bacteria break down plant matter. Many nutrients are not absorbed by the cecum, however, so the chewed food must be expelled, chewed again, and then pass a second time through the intestines. Cecotropes are rich in Vitamin B12, which is essential for a rabbits' health, so once they're expelled through its rectum they're usually immediately re-eaten.

So the rabbit does "chew its cud." Although the modern English word "cud" implies that this already-chewed matter has been regurgitated from a ruminant's stomach directly to its mouth, the original Hebrew word, *gerah*, simply means "chewed food." It doesn't specify the process this *gerah* went through to get back into the rabbit's mouth.

The God who created the rabbit knew this all along. Now you understand why He said that rabbits' meat was unclean.

17

What about the other "errors" in Leviticus 11?

Bible critics say the following verses contain a blatant error: "These are the birds you are to regard as unclean and not eat because they are unclean: the eagle, the vulture, the black vulture. . .and the bat" (Leviticus 11:13, 19 NIV). Most everyone knows that although the bat flies, it's *not* a bird but a mammal. So why does the Bible say it *is?*

In reality, it doesn't. The Hebrew word used here, *oph,* literally means "flyer." Is a bat a flyer? Of course! Most English translations of the Bible use the word "bird"—because all other flyers listed here *are* birds. But it would clear up misunderstandings if they used the more literal word *flyer* instead.

The third "error" in Leviticus 11 is this: "All flying insects that walk on all fours are to be regarded as unclean by you. There are, however, some flying insects that walk on all fours that you may eat: those that have jointed legs for hopping on the ground"

(Leviticus 11:20–21 NIV). It then goes on to list locusts, crickets, and grasshoppers as "clean" insects.

All insects, however, have six legs, not four. If God created insects, the argument goes, surely He would have known how many legs He gave them.

The phrase "walk on all fours" is actually a literary expression—taken from observing common four-footed beasts—and means to walk on the ground as opposed to flying. (Remember, it's talking about *flying* insects here). We use the same expression today. We sometimes say we're "down on all fours" looking for something, even though our hands are technically *not* feet.

The Bible is also making a distinction here between the four normal-sized legs, which are used for nothing but walking, and the larger, hindmost legs of locusts, crickets, and grasshoppers, which, although they're also used for walking, are designed for leaping.

18

How did Moses' staff fit inside the small Ark of the Covenant?

೦ಎ

We know from scripture that the Ark of the Covenant was only about three and three-quarters feet long (Exodus 25:10). (A cubit is eighteen inches, so two and a half cubits equals three and three-quarters feet.) The staff that Moses and Aaron used (Exodus 7:19–20; 17:5–6)—which was a standard shepherd's rod—would have been about five to six feet long (Exodus 3:1; 4:1–4). Yet the Bible tells us the staff was able to fit inside the Ark (Hebrews 9:4). How?

The related question is: Why did God tell Moses he couldn't enter the Promised Land just because he lost his temper once? (We *all* lose our temper at times, right?) Well, when the Israelites first started wandering in the desert, God told Moses to strike a rock with the staff and water would come out. Moses obeyed and water gushed out (Exodus 17:1–7).

Nearly forty years later, God commanded Moses to simply *speak* to a rock and water would flow out.

But Moses, who was very upset with his people at the time, angrily shouted, "Hear now, you rebels! Must we bring water for you out of this rock?" (Numbers 20:10 NKJV). And instead of just speaking to the rock, he whacked it with the staff. . .*twice*! Water gushed out of the rock, but God said that because Moses didn't believe Him and because he didn't respect Him in front of the Israelites, he couldn't lead them into the Promised Land (see Numbers 20:1–13; Deuteronomy 3:23–27; Psalm 106:32–33).

And that was the very last time Moses used the staff.

Have you guessed by now how a wooden rod measuring five to six feet long could fit inside the Ark of the Covenant? Moses apparently struck the staff against the rock with such fury that it broke in two!

19

Haven't archaeologists proved that Jericho wasn't destroyed in Joshua's day?

୬

When Kathleen Kenyon excavated the city mound of Jericho, Tell es-Sultan, from 1952–58, she determined that the level called City IV had been destroyed around 1550 BC. Radiocarbon dates seemed to back up her conclusion.

However, the Exodus was in 1446 BC, so Jericho would have fallen forty years later, in 1406 BC. In fact, archaeologist John Garstrang came to that very conclusion. When he excavated City IV from 1930–36, he found overwhelming proof that it *was* the Jericho of Joshua's day:

(a) Grain storage jars were full of wheat, barley, dates, and lentils, so Garstrang concluded that Jericho IV was destroyed in early spring, after the harvest. This *was* when Joshua besieged Jericho (Joshua 3:15; 5:10).

(b) The fact that the storage jars were full shows that the city wasn't besieged long. Joshua's siege lasted one week (Joshua 6:3–5).

(c) In nearby tombs, Garstrang discovered scarabs of Pharaohs Hatshepsut (1479–58 BC) and Tuthmosis III (1479–25 BC). He found the *same* type of pottery in the tombs as he did in City IV. This dated the pottery of the destroyed city to 1479–25 BC.

(d) Garstrang found pottery painted to imitate Cypriot bichrome style; this is a recognized indication for the Late Bronze Age (1550–1400 BC).

(e) Houses in Jericho IV were built directly against the city wall, just as the Bible describes (Joshua 2:15).

(f) City IV was burned; Garstrang found a layer of charcoal, ashes, and fire-reddened bricks more than three feet thick (Joshua 6:24).

(g) The city wall collapsed right down to the base of the Tell (Joshua 6:20).

There is no doubt that City IV was the Jericho of Joshua's day. This is established by a weight of evidence that simply cannot be ignored—despite Kenyon's opinions and despite radiocarbon dating. Another key event of that period, the eruption of Santorini, also yields radiocarbon dates that vary widely with Egyptian chronology.

20

Weren't Joshua's wars in Canaan just examples of cruel ethnic cleansing?

❧

Canaanite society was so corrupt that God said He was casting them out to make room for the Israelites. In fact, the Canaanites were *so* wicked that the land itself was *vomiting* them out (Leviticus 18:24–25).

God mercifully tried to strike such fear into the Canaanites that those who weren't totally corrupt would flee before Him. That's why He did such tremendous miracles. After God parted the Red Sea and destroyed the chariot armies of Egypt, the most powerful nation on earth, Moses prophesied, "The people will hear and be afraid. . .all the inhabitants of Canaan will melt away. Fear and dread will fall on them" (Exodus 15:14–16 NKJV). And they *did* fear. Rahab told the spies, "Our hearts melted, and no courage remained in any man any longer" (Joshua 2:11 NASB). After God dried the Jordan River "there was no spirit in them any longer" (Joshua 5:1 NKJV). God told the Israelites again and again to "drive them out." He even sent hornets to drive the Canaanites out (Exodus 23:27–31; 34:11; Deuteronomy 7:1). They could have simply fled south to Egypt, and many likely did. In past centuries, tens of thousands of Canaanites *had* migrated to Egypt—and since the Hebrew slaves had left, there was at that very moment a need for laborers.

Sad to say, many Canaanites hardened their hearts and stayed, even though they knew that God Himself, *visibly* traveling with the Israelites (Numbers 14:14), would fight them, even though they knew the Israelites were prepared to wipe them out (Joshua 9:24; 10:1–2). The Canaanites who dug in their heels to fight God Himself brought destruction upon themselves.

21

Did the sun literally stand still in the sky when Joshua prayed for it to?

❧

One day the Amorites surrounded the Israelites' allies at Gibeon, so the Israelites attacked and eventually routed the Amorites. Joshua wanted to finish the battle, so he prayed, "Let the sun stand still over Gibeon, and the moon over the valley of Aijalon." The Bible says, "So the sun stood still and the moon stayed in place until the nation of Israel had defeated its enemies. The sun. . .did not set as on a normal day" (Joshua 10:12–13 NLT).

We know that the sun doesn't orbit the earth but that the earth's rotation makes the sun *appear* to rise and set. So did the world abruptly stop rotating? No. That would have caused global destruction, wiping out all life on earth—the Israelites included. Also, contrary to a popular urban legend, NASA has never discovered "a missing day" in history.

So what really happened at Gibeon? God answered Joshua's prayer, but not the way he'd expected. First of all, the sun was nearly setting when Joshua prayed for it to stand still. (He wouldn't have bothered praying this in the middle of the day with many hours of sunlight still ahead.) Plus, the moon was already shining.

Every day, refraction—in which earth's atmosphere acts like a lens—lengthens daylight by a few minutes. It makes objects appear higher in the sky than they actually are. Refraction causes the sun to be visible moments before it actually rises and causes it to remain "in the sky" for moments after it actually sets below the horizon.

Freakish atmospheric conditions that day caused an extraordinary storm, and more Amorites died when huge hailstones struck them than died in battle (Joshua 10:11). But this event simply cannot be explained by natural phenomena alone. God was evidently manipulating the earth's atmosphere and the laws of nature in a miraculous way.

22

Why does a prominent Israeli archaeologist say that Joshua's conquest never happened?

❧

Israeli archaeologist Israel Finkelstein has demonstrated that around 1200 BC, there was a sudden influx of some twenty-one thousand settlers into the hills of central Canaan. Christians who hold to a "late Exodus" (around 1250 BC) believe these are the Israelites recently come out of Egypt. Finkelstein argues that these newcomers were simply Canaanites who later morphed into the "Israelites." In his opinion, the book of Joshua is a compilation of unrelated "folk memories" about cities destroyed and burned by other peoples at other times.

However, internal evidence shows that the book of Joshua is a historical account, written while eyewitnesses were still living (Joshua 6:25). As we have shown, Jericho *was* destroyed around 1400 BC, and history tells us that around 1400 BC was one of three dates when Hazor was destroyed.

Jericho and Hazor were just about the only cities Joshua destroyed and burned, so we shouldn't expect evidence of Canaan-wide destruction. The Israelites' normal practice was to defeat a Canaanite army then move into the intact cities, houses, and lands (Deuteronomy 6:10–11).

Another point: Joshua 11:16 (NLT) says, "So Joshua conquered the entire region—the hill country, the entire Negev. . .the western foothills, the Jordan Valley, the mountains of Israel, and the Galilean foothills." Yet despite their stunning initial victories, due to later disobedience, the Israelites weren't able to *hold* all this land. Even though they conquered and burned Hazor, within a few decades it was again the center of a Canaanite kingdom (Joshua 11:12–13; Judges 4:1–3). They also conquered Jerusalem, yet it remained a Canaanite stronghold for hundreds more years (Judges 1:8; 2 Samuel 5:6–7; see also Judges 1:19–35).

Even twenty-five years after the conquest, when the Israelites were still largely obedient, God told Joshua that "there remains *very much* land yet to be possessed" (Joshua 13:1 NKJV, emphasis added).

23

Wasn't El (the name for the Hebrew God) originally a Canaanite god?

No. The opposite is true: Much of the ancient Middle East—including the Canaanites—recognized El, the true God, as the Creator God. They recognized El as the original and highest God but early on began to see Him as distant and uncaring. So they developed a mythology in which He spawned seventy sons and daughters who were more accessible.

The world gained a clearer picture of the Canaanite pantheon in 1928, when clay tablets were discovered in Ras Shamra (ancient Ugarit). These tablets described Canaanite beliefs in detail. According to "The Baal Cycle," Baal was chief of the gods under El. Canaanites worshiped Baal most of all, as they believed he had power over essential things such as rain, crops, and fertility. Baal's wife was the goddess Asherah, and Canaanites worshiped them both in lascivious rites.

You can see how tempting it would have been for

the Israelites to turn from worshipping God, El Most High (Genesis 14:19), also called El-Shaddai and Elohim, to worshipping Baal and Asherah—which is exactly what they *did* for much of their history (Judges 3:7; 1 Kings 18:19). This was despite the fact that Moses had commanded them to worship the Lord God (*Yahweh Elohim*) alone, and to utterly demolish the altars and idols of the Canaanite gods (Deuteronomy 12:2–3).

Even when the Israelites worshipped Yahweh, however, they often slipped into syncretism, worshiping Baal, too (1 Kings 18:21). They even assigned Baal's wife to God. An ancient inscription found in Khirbet el-Kom near Hebron, reads: "Blessed be Uriyahu by Yahweh and by his Asherah."

Some people try to cite this to say God has a wife. In reality, all it proves is what the Bible declares: that the Israelites often disobeyed Him by worshipping Asherah, even in the very temple of Yahweh (2 Kings 21:7).

24

What do the Amarna Letters
tell us about the Hebrews in Canaan?

&

The Amarna Letters, discovered in Egypt, are an
archive of clay tablets sent from kings in Canaan to
the Pharaohs. They are basically the Canaanite side
of the story. Written from the 1350s–30s BC, they
contain desperate appeals for Egyptian archers to
stop the attacks of the Habiru/Hapiru, recognizably
the Hebrews. In letter 288, Abdi-Heba, king of
Jerusalem, wrote Pharaoh that "the Hapiru have taken
the very cities of the king," and warned, "If there are
no archers this year, all the lands of the king, my lord,
are lost" (see Judges 1:8).

In the early period of the Judges, following the
death of Joshua, the Israelites in Canaan didn't stand
out too much because they had largely adopted the
Canaanites' housing styles, pottery, customs, and even
their gods. They formed alliances with them (Judges
2:2–3) and even intermarried. "Thus the children
of Israel dwelt among the Canaanites. . . .And they

took their daughters to be their wives, and gave their daughters to their sons; and they served their gods" (Judges 3:5–6 NKJV).

Although they were in danger of becoming assimilated, for the most part they retained their Hebrew identity and resorted to a mixture of warfare against—and alliances with—the Canaanites. Whenever they gained the upper hand, they made the Canaanites pay tribute (Judges 1:28). This is the kind of complex situation that the Amarna Letters describe in the decades following Joshua's death.

One of the most interesting characters was Labayu, ruler of Shechem. Other Canaanites accused him of allying with the Habiru. Abdi-Heba declared that Labayu had handed over Shechem to them. Biridiya, prince of Megiddo, complained that Labayu's sons had hired Habiru mercenaries to war against him. When Labayu wrote Pharaoh, however, he innocently denied knowing that one of his sons consorted with the Habiru.

25

Are there any other proofs that the Israelites lived in Canaan early on?

Early in his reign, Pharaoh Merneptah led a punitive raid into the land of Canaan, and his victory stele (inscribed around 1209 BC) names the cities he conquered. It also states, "Israel is laid waste; its seed is no more." This is the earliest mention of Israel in Egyptian records. This "seed" likely refers to Israel's crops being burned, a common practice at the time. Israel was just a confederation of tribes during the period of the Judges, and Merneptah's stele confirms this. His hieroglyphics specify that Israel was a "foreign people," not a "country."

Also, research by Israeli archaeologist Israel Finkelstein shows that around 1200 BC, less than a decade after the Egyptian raid, there was a sudden influx of some twenty-one thousand people into the central hills of Canaan. Almost overnight, 250 new settlements appeared in these previously uninhabited highlands. The distinctive feature of these settlements was the absence of pig bones—as we know, Israelites were commanded not to eat pork (Leviticus 11:7).

Based upon an Exodus in 1446 BC, 1200 BC was the *exact time* that Midianite hordes began overrunning the plains and valleys of Canaan and Israel.* "Because the power of Midian was so oppressive, the Israelites prepared shelters for themselves in mountain clefts, caves and strongholds" (Judges 6:2 NIV). Many took refuge in the hills and began permanent settlements.

*Jephthah said it had been three hundred years since Israel had conquered the land that Ammon now claimed (Judges 11:25–26). Israel conquered that land in 1406 BC, so Ammon's eighteen-year war began in 1106 BC (Judges 10:8–9). If you add the numbers in Judges 10:3; 10:2; 9:22; 8:28; and 6:1, they take you back ninety-five years from 1106 BC to the beginning of the Midianite raids in 1201 BC. The Israelite retreat to the hills began then.

26

Who was high priest during Saul's reign, Abiathar or Ahimelek?

೩৯

When the Pharisees criticized Jesus and His disciples for "working" on the Sabbath by plucking heads of grain to eat, Jesus replied, "Have you never read what David did when he and his companions were hungry and in need? In the days of Abiathar the high priest, he entered the house of God and ate the consecrated bread" (Mark 2:25–26 NIV).

However, the story Jesus was referring to says, "David went to Nob, to Ahimelek the priest" (1 Samuel 21:1 NIV) and Ahimelek—not his son Abiathar—gave David and his men consecrated bread (1 Samuel 21:2–6). So did Mark make a mistake? Did he misquote Jesus?

After David was at Nob, Saul ordered Ahimelek and his entire extended family (eighty-five priests, all told) to be killed. Only Ahimelek's son Abiathar escaped (1 Samuel 22:9–21). After *that*, yes, Abiathar was high priest. But was he already high priest on the day David arrived there? It seems so.

At that time, Ahimelek and *all* eighty-five men in his extended family were "priests" (1 Samuel 22:11), so calling him "Ahimelek the priest" simply states the obvious. It doesn't mean he was still the *high* priest, the officiating priest. Very likely he was retired from active duty at that point and Abiathar now held the position. That Ahimelek gave David consecrated bread shows that, as former high priest, he still had authority.

A similar situation occurred when the priest Eli was old: his sons Hophni and Phinehas were now the officiating priests, were called the "priests of the LORD" (1 Samuel 1:3 NIV), and were doing the actual sacrifices. Eli was no longer acting high priest, yet he still had the authority to bless the Israelites, and Hannah presented Samuel to Eli, not to his sons (1Samuel 1:17, 25).

27

How could Saul *not* have recognized David, his own armor-bearer?

☙

Many people are mystified when they read King Saul's reaction as David went to fight Goliath. Saul asked his army commander, "Abner, whose son is this youth?" Abner didn't know, so when David came back after killing Goliath, Saul asked, "Whose son are you, young man?" (1 Samuel 17:55, 58 NKJV)

However, in the *previous* chapter, Saul knew David's name, loved him, and had made him his personal armor-bearer. Not only that, but David played music for him whenever he was troubled. How could Saul possibly *not* have recognized David? Bible critics, therefore, say that the sixteenth and seventeenth chapters of 1 Samuel give conflicting accounts of how Saul and David first met.

Some Christians reply that Saul, distressed by a troubling spirit (1 Samuel 16:14), suffered some kind of dementia and couldn't remember who David was. (But Abner, *too*?) The answer, however, had to do with a binding declaration Saul had just made.

Saul had made a vow regarding Goliath: "The man who kills him the king will enrich with great riches, will give him his daughter, and give his father's house exemption from taxes in Israel" (1 Samuel 17:25 NKJV). Saul later gave David his daughter—and probably riches—but he'd also sworn to "give his father's house exemption from taxes." So who *was* his father? Saul needed to know. Note that David answered Saul's question not by giving his *own* name, but by saying, "I am the son of your servant Jesse the Bethlehemite" (1 Samuel 17:58 NKJV).

Previously, Saul had allowed David to go back and forth to his father's house—which is why David had just arrived from Bethlehem—but that now changed (1 Samuel 18:2). David was now in Saul's fulltime employ.

28

What archaeological support has been found for the Bible's accounts of Israel's kings and their wars?

⊱

Archaeology abundantly supports the Bible's accounts of Israel's monarchy and its wars.

The Bible states, "Now Mesha king of Moab raised sheep, and he had to pay the king of Israel a tribute of a hundred thousand lambs and the wool of a hundred thousand rams. But after Ahab died, the king of Moab rebelled against the king of Israel. So at that time King Joram set out from Samaria and mobilized all Israel" (2 Kings 3:4–6 NIV).

In 1868, the Mesha Stele was found in Jordan. It is Mesha's account of his rebellion, dedicated to his god, Chemosh. It states, in part: "I am Mesha, son of Kemosh, king of Moab. And I built this high place to Kemosh to commemorate deliverance from all the kings. . . . Omri was king of Israel, and he oppressed Moab for many days. . .and his son [Ahab] replaced him; and he also said, 'I will oppress Moab.' But I was victorious over him and his house."

Also, the Bible states that Ben-Hadad was king of Aram, that the prophet Elisha anointed Hazael king, and that Hazael then assassinated Ben-Hadad and ruled in his place (2 Kings 8:7–15). An inscription by Shalmaneser, king of Assyria says, "I fought with Ben-Hadad. I accomplished his defeat. Hazael, son of a nobody, seized his throne."

Other Assyrian monuments add new details that dovetail with what the Bible tells us: Jehoram was the grandson of Omri (1 Kings 16:29; 2 Kings 3:1) and the Black Obelisk, found in Shalmaneser's palace, states: "The tribute of Iaua mar Hu-umrii [Jehoram son of Omri]: I have received from him silver, gold, a bowl of gold, chalices of gold, tumblers of gold, buckets of gold, tin, a scepter for the king, and spears." [Some believe *Iaua* was Jehu, who slew Jehoram and was the next king of Israel (2 Kings 9)].

29

Does Psalm 137 say evil men should be *happy* as they kill infants?

കം

This passage has long disturbed believers: "Daughter Babylon, doomed to destruction, happy is the one who repays you according to what you have done to us. Happy is the one who seizes your infants and dashes them against the rocks" (Psalm 137:8–9 NIV).

In Jeremiah's day, Israel had rebelled against God so He allowed the Babylonians to attack them. Jeremiah wept in anguish as his people were slain and their children collapsed from hunger (Lamentations 2:11). The Lord had sent the Babylonians to judge the people of Israel for their sins, but their excessive cruelty was *not* part of His plan. God said, "I was angry with my chosen people and punished them by letting them fall into your hands. But you, Babylon, showed them no mercy" (Isaiah 47:6 NLT).

The Babylonians then mercilessly demanded that the grieving exiles entertain them with happy songs: "our tormentors demanded songs of joy" (Psalm

137:3 NIV). The point of this psalm is that just as the Babylonian tormentors got perverse pleasure from slaying the Jews and then forcing the traumatized survivors to sing joyful tunes, *their* enemies would get a twisted sense of happiness out of slaying them—men, women, and children. Warfare back then was barbaric and cruel, and the defenseless and innocent weren't spared (2 Kings 8:12).

God didn't desire Babylon's enemies to be that cruel, let alone be happy doing it. The psalmist was simply repeating what the prophet Isaiah had said those enemies *would* do: "A prophecy against Babylon. . . . Their infants will be dashed to pieces before their eyes. . . . I will stir up against them the Medes. . . . Their bows will strike down the young men; they will have no mercy on infants" (Isaiah 13:1, 16–18 NIV).

The Babylonians were ruthless and cruel, and God knew that their enemies were just as ruthless and cruel as they were.

30

What does the Bible really say about the shape of the earth?

❧

Some skeptics believe the Bible says the world is flat with four corners. That, they say, is proof that the Bible wasn't inspired by God (who, according to them, probably doesn't exist anyway) but was written by mere men with primitive, unscientific worldviews. The problem with this position, however, is that nowhere does the Bible *say* the world is flat. This *was* the general worldview of people of that day, and the Hebrews may have had this misconception. But it isn't stated in the Bible. In fact, the scriptures taught way back in 700 BC that the world is round:

"Have you not known? Have you not heard? Has it not been told you from the beginning? Have you not understood from the foundations of the earth? It is He who sits above the circle of the earth, and its inhabitants are like grasshoppers" (Isaiah 40:21–22 NKJV). A circle is as round as things get.

As for the Mesopotamian belief that the world

was a raft floating on the waters, the Bible stated this scientific reality in 1,500 BC: "He [God] spreads out the northern skies over empty space; he suspends the earth over nothing" (Job 26:7 NIV).

Still, the critics argue, the Bible *does* mention "the four corners of the earth" (Isaiah 11:12 KJV). However, the Hebrew word translated "corners" is *kanaph*, which literally means "wings." Clearly, this is symbolic language used to describe the four directions—north, south, east, and west. The same word is used in Ezekiel 7:2 (KJV), which refers to "the four corners of the land" of Israel. Yet no critics would argue that the Israelites believed their country was a square, or that there were four giant wings on the borders of their nation.

31

What, if anything, does the Bible say about life on other planets— or other solar systems or galaxies?

When God created our sun and planet, "he made the stars also" (Genesis 1:16 KJV). Astronomers estimate that there are 200 billion to 400 billion stars in our Milky Way Galaxy alone. And they guesstimate that there are some 170 billion galaxies in the universe. You do the math—that's a *lot* of stars! It shows us how astonishingly creative God really is.

Scientists have discovered hundreds of planets orbiting nearby stars and calculate that odds are our galaxy has some 50 billion planets, of which 500 million are within the habitable zone of their star. Now, if 500 million planets (just in our galaxy) can potentially support life, isn't it reasonable to believe that the Planet Earth just might not be the only inhabited world? Are we so special after all?

Some note that God "stretches out the heavens. . . like a tent to dwell in" (Isaiah 40:22 NKJV) and argue that He expressly created habitable planets like earth to be inhabited (Isaiah 45:18). But we still can't say for sure whether or not life exists elsewhere. But if it *does* exist, it was God (through Jesus Christ) who created it: "All things were made through Him, and without Him nothing was made that was made" (John 1:3 NKJV).

This brings up another question: If there *is* life elsewhere in the universe, is it fallen like earth's humanity and in need of salvation? As some have asked, "Did Jesus die for Klingons too?" Well, we can't know whether or not hypothetical beings on other planets are fallen. But we *do* know that every sentient being in existence will one day worship Jesus: "that at the name of Jesus every knee should bow, of those in heaven, and of those on earth. . .and that every tongue should confess that Jesus Christ is Lord" (Philippians 2:10–11 NKJV).

The planet Earth may or may not be unique in its ability to support life—but Jesus Christ is *definitely* unique!

32

Why do Matthew and Luke give different genealogies for Jesus?

Matthew listed Jesus' ancestors at the beginning of his Gospel. This was important, because he was writing for a Jewish audience, and the Jews knew that the Messiah would be descended from King David. Matthew's purpose of including Jesus' pedigree was to confirm that He *was* "the Son of David" (Matthew 1:1 NKJV).

Matthew gave Jesus' lineage beginning with Abraham, but Luke, who was a Gentile, traced Jesus' lineage all the way back to Adam to show His link with *all* humanity. From Abraham to David, the two lists are almost exactly the same. However, beginning with King David, they list *very* different ancestors. Compare these:

David, Solomon, Rehoboam, Abijah, Asa, Jehoshaphat, etc. (Matthew 1:6–8)

David, Nathan, Mattathah, Menan, Melea, Eliakim, etc. (Luke 3:30–31)

The lists continue to differ all the way down the line to Joseph's immediate ancestors:

Achim, Eliud, Eleazar, Matthan, Jacob, Joseph (Matthew 1:14–16)

Janna, Melchi, Levi, Matthat, Heli, Joseph (Luke 3:23–24)

Why the differences? Well, Matthew, following required Jewish format, listed the genealogy of Jesus' earthly father Joseph—even though he went on to state that Joseph was *not* Jesus' natural, biological father (Matthew 1:18). Note that all the royal kings of Judah were Joseph's ancestors. He was not only of the *lineage* of David, but of the "*house* and lineage of David" (Luke 2:4 NKJV, emphasis added).

But for Jesus to be physically descended from King David, and not simply be adopted by one of his descendants, His mother Mary *also* had to be "of the lineage of David." And she was. Jews didn't cite women's genealogies, but Mary's father, Heli, kept track of *his*, and he (and therefore Mary) was *also* descended from David, through one of David's younger sons, Nathan (1 Chronicles 3:5). It is therefore Mary's genealogy that Luke records.

33

Were huge crowds of followers and fans a danger to Jesus?

و&

Jesus was so wildly popular during His earthly ministry that crowd control was sometimes a serious issue. Often when He was in a house or went walking in public, people crowded thickly around Him (Mark 2:1–2; 5:24). It got to be such a problem that after a while He could no longer openly enter certain cities (Mark 1:45).

Jesus had a tremendous reputation as a healer, so people who were sick pushed and pressed through packed crowds so they could touch Him and be healed (Mark 3:10). At one point "a great multitude, when they heard how many things He was doing, came to Him. So He told His disciples that a small boat should be kept ready for Him because of the multitude, lest they should crush Him" (Mark 3:8–9 NKJV).

Got that? Jesus stood with His back to the lake, facing the crowds ringing Him on the shore, with a small boat behind Him. Probably a couple disciples stood beside this boat and "kept ready" to launch out. In case the crowd got too excited and impatient and all surged forward to touch Him at once, Jesus had an escape plan: He would jump into the boat and push out to sea.

At one point, that's what He did. Before He had twelve disciples to help with crowd control, Jesus was teaching and "great crowds pressed in on him to listen to the word of God." As a precautionary measure, Jesus got into Simon Peter's boat and had him push out a ways from the shore (Luke 5:1–3 NLT).

It wasn't just Jesus they nearly crushed, but each other. One time, "an innumerable multitude of people had gathered together, so that they trampled one another" (Luke 12:1 NKJV). Hopefully, only people's toes got trampled.

34

How long after Jesus' death and resurrection were the Gospels written?

Many scholars state that none of the Gospels was written before AD 70, some forty years after Jesus ascended back to heaven. This is based upon two assumptions: (a) the Romans destroyed Jerusalem in AD 70, but skeptics argue that the Gospels containing Jesus' prophecies about that event (Matthew 24:1–2; Luke 21:20–24) must have been composed *after* the fact. (b) As to why Matthew (an eyewitness) and Luke (who interviewed eyewitnesses) would have waited so long to write their narratives, critics insist that others actually penned their Gospels.

However, church tradition attributes the first three Gospels to Matthew, Mark, and Luke and states that they were written early. Internal evidence points to the same. For example, Luke's Gospel and the book of Acts are both dedicated to Theophilus (Luke 1:3; Acts 1:1). Now, we know that Luke wrote Acts before AD 62, when Paul was released from his first imprisonment, because the book ends with Paul still under house arrest (Acts 28:30–31).

In Acts, Luke refers to his "former book" (Acts 1:1 NIV). He therefore likely wrote his gospel before AD 60. Luke also states that "many" had written Gospels before him (Luke 1:1), so Mark and Matthew also likely would have been written before AD 60.

Matthew's Gospel was written for Jews, and "Matthew, who had at first preached to the Hebrews, when he was about to go to other peoples, committed his Gospel to writing" (Eusebius, *Ecclesiastical History*, Book 3, Chapter 24).

The apostles were still in Jerusalem in AD 49–50, because Acts 15:2, 4, and 6 tell us that the "apostles and elders" met Paul then. However, when Paul went to Jerusalem in AD 57, he met "James, and all the elders" (Acts 21:17–18 NIV) but no apostles. They had left to fulfill the Great Commission. So Matthew composed his Gospel around AD 50–56.

35

Which Gospel was written first—Matthew or Mark?

൭

The church fathers believed that Matthew wrote his Gospel first and that Mark edited down Matthew's work to the bare-bones story. However, it's likely that Mark was closer to the original story since in places the sense of the underlying Aramaic words shows through in his Greek text.

Mark is the shortest Gospel of the four. It focuses on the basic story of Jesus with almost none of the parables or stories found in Matthew and Luke. Mark is only 661 verses long, yet 606 of those verses (often quoted word for word) are found in Matthew. In other words, 92 percent of Mark appears in Matthew. In addition, 350 verses from Mark appear with little change in Luke. That is why many Bible scholars believe that Matthew and Luke based their Gospels on Mark's text. This theory is called "Markan priority."

However, it's unlikely that the task of first

organizing and writing Jesus' biography would have been left to Mark, since Jesus had appointed twelve apostles whose time was devoted "continually to. . . the ministry of the word" (Acts 6:2, 4 NKJV). Mark was not among the Twelve. *They* knew the facts best and had been commissioned to bear witness to Christ (Acts 1:21–22). Very likely, the apostles wrote down the basic framework of Jesus' words and deeds early on, and then Mark, Matthew, and Luke all independently based their Gospels on *this* original document, with Matthew and Luke adding more of Jesus' sayings and parables from other sources.

What other sources? Papias (AD 70–163) wrote, "Matthew compiled the *Logia* in the Hebrew [that is, Aramaic] speech, and everyone translated them as best he could." *Logia* means "oracles," and this is thought to refer to an original Aramaic collection of Jesus' sayings and parables. Scholars commonly call this "Q" for the German word *quelle*, which means "source."

36

Why do some people believe the Gospels were based on already-written records?

It makes eminent sense that when Matthew, Mark, and Luke wrote their Gospels, they based them on an already-written story framework to which they added stories, quotes, and parables from a second written resource (commonly called Q). John did not use that framework when he wrote his Gospel but drew heavily from *other* written sources.

Many Christians hesitate to believe in Q because it's often endorsed by unbelieving scholars. Yet the existence of a written collection of sayings would ensure the accuracy and inerrancy of the Bible's text. If there wasn't an early written record of Jesus' sayings, how could Matthew—some twenty-five years later—quote lengthy chunks of Jesus' sayings in chapters 5, 6, and 7? And how could John—some sixty years after Jesus' death, burial, resurrection, and ascension—quote Jesus verbatim in chapters 14, 15, 16, and 17? It's important that we have the *actual* words of Jesus in passages such as John 14:6—not half-remembered summaries or paraphrases.

Now, some Jews could, over a period of years, memorize large portions of the Law—but they had a written text to constantly refer to. How do you memorize a sermon, though, while someone's *giving* it? Some Christians quote Jesus' promise that the Holy Spirit would "bring to your remembrance all things that I said to you" (John 14:26 NKJV). They believe God did a miracle each time the apostles sat down to write. That's possible. Nevertheless, reusable wax-covered writing tablets existed long before AD 30, as did professional scribes trained to take notes in shorthand.

Of all Jesus' apostles, who was most likely that scribe? Matthew, of course, since he'd been an official tax collector for the Romans—a job that required him to be fluent in both Greek and Aramaic, and to write down very accurate, detailed records.

37

When did the disciples first *know* that Jesus was the Messiah and the Son of God?

One day, John the Baptist's disciples heard him declare that Jesus was the Lamb of God and the Messiah (John 1:29–36). Two of those disciples then spent hours talking with Jesus. Andrew came away so impressed that he told his brother Simon, "We have found the Messiah." The next day, Nathanael exclaimed, "Rabbi, you are the Son of God—the King of Israel!" (John 1:41, 49 NLT). Bible scholars tell us this happened in the fall of AD 26, at the beginning of Jesus' ministry.

However, in the spring of AD 29, when Simon Peter declared, "You are the Christ, the Son of the living God," Jesus said, "Blessed are you, Simon Bar-Jonah, for flesh and blood has not revealed this to you, but My Father who is in heaven" (Matthew 16:16–17 NKJV). *That* sounds like Simon Peter was the *first* to realize Jesus was the Christ, and only after having been with Him for two and a half years. So which Gospel is right?

Both are. In Jesus' day, Jews eagerly expected the arrival of the Messiah, and Jesus' disciples followed Him because they believed He was the One. Even the crowds speculated that He was the Messiah (John 7:25–26, 31, 40–41). To avoid being mobbed by admirers or stoned by enemies, however, Jesus refrained from publicly declaring His true identity, leading many people to wonder just *who* He was (Matthew 16:13–14).

Because Jesus wasn't working to overthrow the Roman government, like many Jews thought the Messiah would, John the Baptist—who had called Jesus the Messiah—asked, "Are you the Messiah we've been expecting, or should we keep looking for someone else?" (Matthew 11:3 NLT).

Even many of Jesus' disciples gave up hope, but Simon declared, "We have come to believe and to know that you are the Holy One of God" (John 6:69 NIV). Then Simon Peter's declaration three months later (in Matthew 16) was a reaffirmation of the disciples' unswerving faith in Jesus.

38

Did the early church deliberately
change the original Greek words
to make Jesus look better?

In his book *Misquoting Jesus*, Bart Ehrman presents
Mark 1:41 as proof that editors deliberately
doctored the text. In question are the Greek words
splangnistheis ("feeling compassion") and *orgistheis*
("becoming angry"). In almost every Greek
manuscript, *splangnistheis* appears in Mark 1:41.
Thus, most Bibles read that Jesus "felt compassion"
when a leper came to Him saying, "If you are
willing, you can make me clean" (Mark 1:40 NIV).
As the 1984 version of the NIV reads, "Filled with
compassion, Jesus reached out his hand and touched
the man."

But in *one* Greek manuscript, Codex Bezae, the
word *orgistheis* appears, so that when the leper asked
Jesus to heal him, Jesus became angry. . .*then* healed
him. Wanting to reflect the "original" Greek text, the
2011 version of the NIV reads, "Jesus was indignant.

He reached out his hand and touched the man."

It frankly makes no difference to our understanding of Jesus' nature which word was original. We can certainly understand Jesus having compassion on a poor leper (Matthew 14:14; 20:34). On the other hand, Mark doesn't hesitate to show Jesus becoming indignant or angry on other occasions (Mark 3:5; 10:14).

However, there's such a difference between *orgistheis* and *splangnistheis* that critics argue that the text was blatantly changed to make Jesus look better. Actually, it's more likely that it's an innocent scribal error. A Jewish Christian fluent in both Aramaic and Greek, when copying Mark's Gospel, would have realized that the underlying Aramaic word *ethra'em* (He was enraged) is very easily confused with *ethraham* (He had pity). Concluding that a translation error had been made, he changed the Greek word accordingly.

After examining all the evidence, Dr. Daniel B. Wallace, an evangelical New Testament Studies professor at Dallas Theological Seminary, came to believe that the case is strong for Jesus having pity, but that the evidence weighs slightly more towards Jesus being angry. (For more information, see the online NET Bible.)

39

Why do some events appear in different order in the Gospels?

಄

Bible students have realized for two thousand years that although Matthew, Mark, and Luke often relate the same incidents in the same order, they don't *always* do so.

For example, Matthew's Gospel relates these events in *this* order: (1) Jesus calls Matthew to follow; (2) He heals a woman and raises a dead girl; (3) He heals the man with a withered hand (Matthew 9:9–13,18–26; 12:9–14). Mark, however, relates the same events in *this* order: (1) Jesus calls Matthew to follow; (2) He heals the man with a withered hand; (3) He heals a woman and raises a dead girl (Mark 2:13–17; 3:1–6; 5:21–43).

The major events of Jesus' ministry are in the same chronological order, but sometimes the minor incidents have been arranged in different orders.

What is more amazing is that when the Gospels relate the same incident or saying, they repeat it almost word for word—sometimes *exactly* word for word (compare Matthew 3:7–10 with Luke 3:7–9.) This is why Matthew, Mark, and Luke are called the Synoptic Gospels. The word *synoptic* means "seen together." The first three gospels are called the Synoptic Gospels because they contain so many parallel texts.

These short, self-contained stories are called *pericopes*, a Greek word that means "a cutting out." It appears that these pericopes were written and compiled early on and that the Gospel writers then chose the stories they wanted—generally following the same timeline, but sometimes rearranging the material for editorial purposes, to suit their intended audience. In a sense, this *is* what happened, but God guided the process.

As the church father Tertullian (AD 160–220) said, "Never mind if there does occur some variation in the order of their narratives, provided that there be agreement in the essential matter of the faith" (*Against Marcion*, IV, 2).

40

How accurate are the Gospel
accounts of the words Jesus said?

&

Often when the Synoptic Gospels relate the same
incident, they give different details. This is to be
expected and is not a problem, as these are just
different views of the same event. Sometimes,
however, the Gospels vary slightly as to what Jesus
said. The meaning of what He says is the same, but
the words used are sometimes a bit different. So the
question some people ask is this: Do the Gospels
record the *exact* words Jesus said, or only a close
approximation?

For example, when Jesus and the apostles were
caught in the middle of a storm so terrible that the
Twelve thought they were about to perish, Jesus
rebuked the wind and the waves—which instantly
calmed. Matthew tells us that after Jesus calmed the
storm, He asked, "You of little faith, why are you so
afraid?" (Matthew 8:26 NIV). Mark reports that He
asked, "Why are you so afraid? Do you still have no

faith?" (Mark 4:40 NIV), while Luke tells us that Jesus asked simply, "Where is your faith?" (Luke 8:25 NIV).

A careful reading of all three stories, however, shows that Jesus asked the question in Matthew just *before* He calmed the storm. Then, *after* he'd done the miracle He asked, "Why are you so afraid? Do you still have no faith?" Since the disciples were too astonished to answer Him, it's easy to see Jesus sadly asking again, "Where is your faith?"

The differences in what the disciples shouted to Jesus are easy to explain. There were, after all, twelve of them in the boat with Jesus and they believed they were in terrible danger and were frightened out of their wits. They undoubtedly said all the things Matthew, Mark, and Luke record them saying, and probably quite a bit more as well (Matthew 8:25; Mark 4:38; Luke 8:24).

41

Did Jesus preach the Sermon on the Mount on a hilltop or down on a plain?

Many people wonder why there are differences between Matthew's and Luke's accounts of the famous "Sermon on the Mount." Here's how each of them begin:

- "Now when [Jesus] saw the crowds, he went up on a mountainside and sat down. His disciples came to him, and he began to teach them. He said: 'Blessed are the poor in spirit, for theirs is the kingdom of heaven'" (Matthew 5:1–3 NIV).
- "He went down with them and stood on a level place. A large crowd of his disciples was there and a great number of people. . . . Looking at his disciples, he said: 'Blessed are you who are poor, for yours is the kingdom of God'" (Luke 6:17, 20 NIV).

Matthew tells us Jesus was sitting on a mountainside, while Luke says He was standing on a plain. In addition, Luke reports that Jesus gave this sermon immediately after choosing the twelve apostles, whereas in Matthew's gospel, Jesus didn't choose His apostles until *several* chapters after this sermon. Also, although they both begin with the Beatitudes, Matthew's version is much longer, stretching out over three chapters. Luke not only omits much material, but he scatters parts of it throughout his Gospel (see Luke 11:2–4; 12:22–31, 33–34).

Finally, Jesus' wording, although similar in Matthew and Luke, has many striking differences, as even His brief opening words show.

There is no need to attempt to harmonize them into one event. The multi-subject Sermon on the Mount in Matthew 5–7 is commonly understood to be the *heart* of Jesus' teaching. Therefore, as He traveled around Judea and Galilee, He would have repeated these core messages again and again, to new crowds in different towns, villages, and open-air settings. Yes, He taught *other* principles and told *other* parables as well, but these were probably some of His most oft-repeated teachings.

42

Why does Luke give the wrong date for when Quirinius was governor?

&

Luke wrote, "In those days Caesar Augustus issued a decree that a census should be taken of the entire Roman world. (This was the first census that took place while Quirinius was governor of Syria.)" (Luke 2:1–2 NIV). Jesus was born in 4 BC, so Caesar's decree would have happened then. The problem, however, is that Quirinius was governor of Syria from AD 6–9, when he conducted a census, which was so unpopular that it sparked a Jewish revolt (Acts 5:37).

Pope Gregory XIII's aides made a mistake when calculating our modern calendar. We now know that Jesus was born four years earlier—hence He was actually born in 4 BC. Some people wonder if Luke also got his dates mixed up, or his information wrong.

The Greek for this passage literally reads, "*This enrollment first was governing Syria Cyrenius.*" Therefore, the NIV footnotes suggest an alternate translation: "This census took place before Quirinius was governor of Syria." In other words, Luke—who wrote both the Gospel of Luke and the book of Acts—was clarifying for his readers that this was *not* the more recent census under Quirinius but an earlier one.

Many Christians, however, believe that Quirinius was possibly Governor of Syria *twice*—first in 4 BC and again in AD 6–9—and that he conducted a census both times. History is silent on whether Quirinius was governor of Syria twice, but it seems unlikely.

One thing that seems certain is that no surviving Roman records speak of an empire-wide census taking place in 4 BC. But did such records once exist? The Latin Church Father Tertullian (AD 160–220) says that this earlier census indeed took place, and that it was documented in the archives in Rome (*Against Marcion* 4:7). These records no longer exist, but according to Tertullian, they were extant in his day.

Luke's accuracy has been questioned when his accounts disagreed with those of historians, but every time, new archaeological evidence vindicated his statements.

43

Why does John's Gospel differ
so much from the other Gospels?
Is it a later forgery?

❧

John's Gospel doesn't recount several of the events of Jesus' life found in the other Gospels, plus it recounts many incidents and conversations the Synoptic Gospels don't. But John doesn't contradict Matthew, Mark, or Luke. Rather, his Gospel is a rich source of information that fills in many gaps in the story and greatly clarifies the timeline.

John emphasizes the deity of Christ to a much greater extent than the other Gospel writers. While this theme *is* found in the Synoptics, John boldly states that "the Word was God" and "the Word became flesh" (John 1:1, 14 NIV). St. Jerome wrote that one of the reasons John wrote his Gospel was to counter the heresies of the Ebionites—who taught that Jesus was the Messiah but was the natural son of Joseph who *became* the Son of God at His baptism.

John's Gospel is believed to have been written

around AD 85–90. Scholars once argued that its theology was so developed that someone else pretending to be an eyewitness must have written it much later. But in 1920, a fragment of the Gospel of John (the *Rylands Library Papyrus P52*), which dated to AD 117–138, was found. If copies already existed then, the original must date even earlier. Also, the author *was* very familiar with Jewish customs and Judea's geography.

John 21:20, 24 state that "the disciple whom Jesus loved" wrote this gospel, and John was one of Jesus' three closest disciples (Mark 9:2; 14:32–33).

The Muratorian Fragment, dated to AD 170, states that John's fellow disciples urged him to write a Gospel. John was at first hesitant, but eventually agreed to do so if they reviewed it. This is confirmed by the "we" in the following: "This is the disciple who testifies to these things and who wrote them down. We know that his testimony is true" (John 21:24 NIV).

44

Is Mark 16:9–20 the original ending to the Gospel of Mark?

∂

Mark 16:6–7 reports that after the women who had followed Jesus discovered the stone rolled away from His tomb, an angel told them that He had risen from the dead and to go tell His disciples. Then Mark 16:8 (NKJV) states, "So they went out quickly and fled from the tomb, for they trembled and were amazed. And they said nothing to anyone, for they were afraid."

And there, according to many scholars, the Gospel of Mark ends. In some Bible translations, such as the New International Version, the following note appears: "[The earliest manuscripts and some other ancient witnesses do not have verses 9–20.]" By "the earliest manuscripts," they mean the Codex Vaticanus and Codex Siniaticus, dated around AD 350. However, it seems highly unlikely that Mark would have deliberately ended his gospel on such an abrupt note. On the other hand, verses 9–14 and 19–20 *do* read like a summary tacked on the end to bring a conclusion where one was lacking. Mary Magdalene is mentioned in verse 1, yet is *re*introduced in verse 9 with information that echoes Luke 8:2.

It is likely that Mark originally had a different ending but that it was lost—or possibly the end of the sheet of papyrus broke off. So an editor compiled information from other sources and penned a brief ending. Why not? We know that godly men were later inspired to add editorial notes to the Law of Moses, and we don't think anything amiss—so why should we find it disingenuous that a Christian editor should do the same?

The inspired editor clearly had access to original documents, as evidenced by the sayings of Jesus he quoted in Mark 16:15–18. This process was nothing new. For example, Luke did not write his Gospel by direct revelation; he composed it from already-existing material and eyewitness testimony, which he judiciously arranged and edited.

45

Why do some believe that the story of the woman caught in adultery should not be part of the Bible?

The story of the woman caught in adultery (also known as the *Pericope Adulterae*) is a well-known and much-loved passage found in our Bible translations today. It's so in keeping with the religious confrontations of Jesus' day, His forgiveness, and His command to lead a godly life that it's hard for many to believe that it wasn't originally part of John's Gospel. Yet for decades, Bible versions such as the NIV contained this disclaimer: "[The earliest manuscripts and many other ancient witnesses do not have John 7:53– 8:11.]"

The four earliest manuscripts, P66 and P75 (from the AD 200s) and Codex Siniaticus and Codex Vaticanus (from around AD 350), don't contain it—although they *do* contain diacritical (editorial) marks in their margins acknowledging the existence of the excluded story. However, the Didascalia (AD 230) mentions it, and Didymus the Blind (AD 313–398) reported that the story was found in several copies. Augustine (AD 354–430) argued that it was authentic but that it had been excluded by editors who feared that it gave women license to commit adultery.

So is this passage inspired scripture? The evangelical New Testament scholar Dr. Daniel B. Wallace, while researching New Testament manuscripts in Albania, found that the story was lacking in three of the texts, and was in an entirely different place in a fourth manuscript—at the *end* of John's Gospel. He therefore believes that it was *not* originally part of the biblical text.

Other scholars believe the story is scriptural. They reason that although it wasn't originally part of John's text, the early church recognized it as an authentic story and therefore added it to his Gospel. They probably chose to add it at *this* spot because that's when the incident happened. Notice that a few verses later Jesus said, "I pass judgment on no one" (John 8:15 NIV).

46

How many differences are there between the various Greek manuscripts?

The two previous Q&A's refer to the largest and best-known differences in the ancient New Testament texts, but there are many thousands of minor variations (called "textual variants") in the Greek texts. This has caused some skeptics to assert that there are *so many* differences that we can never truly know what the *original* text actually said. But this is a deliberately exaggerated view, one the actual evidence does not warrant.

There are two reasons for the large number of textual variants. First, they not only include accidental omissions and additions, but also tiny variations in spelling or different arrangements of the same words, even though such differences almost never alter the meaning of the text. In other words, even the most insignificant differences count as variants—and the overwhelming majority of these differences *are* insignificant. They don't affect any important Christian doctrine.

Second, there are more than fifty-five hundred copies of Greek New Testament manuscripts in existence. (This doesn't even include ten thousand Latin manuscripts or five thousand manuscripts in other ancient languages.) While the majority of these Greek texts come from later centuries, about twelve come from the AD 100s, sixty-four date back to the AD 200s, and forty-eight copies were made in the AD 300s. Together, these early copies contain the complete New Testament several times over. The New Testament is the best-attested book from the ancient world.

Can we be certain that the scriptures we have today are the same as the original New Testament? Yes, we can! After comparing the various copies, and by sifting out the countless insignificant variations, scholars (and we) have an excellent idea of what the original autographs of the New Testament really said.

47

Which Greek manuscripts are the most accurate New Testament texts?

ॐ

First of all, it's important to know that most New Testament manuscripts belong to one of three textual "families." The differences between these textual groups cause both scholars and laypeople to advocate one above another. This dispute goes back sixteen hundred years.

For example, the Old Latin translations, including the Latin Vulgate, are based upon a text that has come to be called the Western Text. When Jerome produced the Vulgate around AD 400, he also had access to the Byzantine Text (of Lucian of Antioch) and the Alexandrian Text (of Hesychius of Egypt), but he spoke disparagingly of both. Thus, the Western Text, through Jerome's Latin translation, dominated Western Europe from about AD 400 until the 1500s.

During this same time, Christians of the Greek-speaking Byzantine Empire continued using the

Byzantine Text. After Constantinople fell in 1453, some of these manuscripts were brought to the West, where in 1515 a Dutch scholar named Erasmus compiled them into one text (later called the *Textus Receptus*—meaning "Received Text"). Martin Luther's New Testament and the King James Bible are based upon this text, and it dominated the Christian world for 450 years.

Then, in the 1800s, scholars discovered the *Codex Siniaticus*; plus the *Codex Vaticanus* was made public. Both copies were produced around AD 350 and mostly represent the Alexandrian Text. Once again, the "new" readings were compiled into one text, which scholars believed was the most accurate version. Most modern Bible translations are largely based on this text.

So which text is most accurate? While some people exclusively favor one text and speak disparagingly of all others, many scholars believe that *all* these texts have an important part to contribute. It's worth noting that there are far more differences in our modern Bibles due to translation styles than to differences in the original Greek texts.

48

How reliable are biblical accounts of Jesus' miracles?

&

One of the premises of what has come to be called "higher criticism" is that only the Bible's historical and plausible statements are to be accepted—and *then* only after being reinterpreted and adjusted. All miracles and supernatural events are automatically dismissed as later embellishments. In their search for the "real, historical Jesus," skeptics typically view the biblical texts as falsified and unreliable—except when a verse lines up with their views.

At least you have to give them credit for acknowledging that Jesus *existed*. Some decades ago, it was popular to state that the Church had invented myths about a man called Jesus. But the evidence of Jesus' existence, even in secular history, is too strong, and critics were eventually forced to bow to the facts. Today, no credible historian denies that Jesus lived.

As for miracles, if you believe that God created the world and that Jesus told the truth when He claimed to be God's Son, then certainly He had the power to do miracles—yes, even to raise the dead, calm a raging storm, and walk on the sea. Miracles often contradict the normal laws of nature, but that doesn't make them impossible. After all, God created the laws of nature in the first place, so He's able to supersede them when He desires. As Jesus said, "The things which are impossible with men are possible with God" (Luke 18:27 KJV).

Jesus did healing miracles because, in a day when doctors were few and medicine rudimentary, the fact that He healed people showed that God loved them. His miracles also demonstrated God's power and proved that He was the Messiah (Luke 7:19–22). Jesus' many miracles finally culminated in His greatest miracle of all—when He rose from the dead. This, the apostle Paul wrote, was the definitive proof that Jesus was God's Son (Romans 1:3–4).

49

Did Jesus heal one blind man as He entered Jericho or two blind men as He left?

❧

Jesus and His disciples, with a large crowd following them, were walking to Jerusalem when, near Jericho, two blind men heard the excitement and asked what was happening. When the crowd told them Jesus was passing through, the blind men cried out to Him to have mercy on them. The crowd sternly told them to be quiet, but they shouted even louder, so Jesus called them and asked what they wanted. When they replied that they wished to receive their sight, He immediately healed them.

The details in all three Synoptic Gospels correspond *so* closely that it's clear they're all referring to the same incident. However, there are differences.

Luke tells us, "As Jesus was approaching Jericho, a blind man was sitting by the road" (Luke 18:35 NASB). Matthew says, "As they were leaving Jericho. . . two blind men [were] sitting by the road" (Matthew

20:29–30 NASB). Mark agrees with Matthew that this happened "as He was leaving Jericho" but tells of only *one* blind man, named Bartimaeus (Mark 10:46–47 NASB).

As Matthew states, there were *two* blind men. But Mark focused only on Bartimaeus since he was the best-known of the two.

As for *where* this miracle happened, since most of the details are identical, it's unlikely that Jesus healed one blind man as He entered Jericho and two more as He left. The answer is found in the fact that the *old* city of Jericho was almost uninhabited in Jesus' day and that King Herod had built a *new* city of Jericho a mile to the south. Jesus and His disciples had apparently stopped at the old city to rest then continued on to the new city.

In Bible times, beggars normally sat just outside a city's gates. These blind men had wisely positioned themselves further away, "by the road," so they could be first in line for travelers' charity.

50

Why do the Gospels give three different dates for Jesus driving the merchants from the temple?

❧

Matthew tells us that after riding into Jerusalem in His Triumphal Entry, "Jesus entered the temple courts and drove out all who were buying and selling there. He overturned the tables of the money changers and the benches of those selling doves" (Matthew 21:12 NIV). Then He went to Bethany for the night. The next morning, as He returned to Jerusalem, He cursed a fig tree (Matthew 21:17–19). Luke agrees with Matthew's order of events (Luke 19:28–46).

Mark, however, tells us that after Jesus rode into Jerusalem and entered the temple area, He apparently just "looked around" before heading to Bethany. The next morning, He cursed the fig tree *then* cleansed the temple (Mark 11:1–17).

Now, John doesn't mention Jesus clearing out the temple in AD 30, but tells us He did so three years *earlier* (John 2:13–16). These are clear contradictions, aren't they?

No, they're not. Jesus cleared out the temple at least *twice*. On the first occasion, the Jews said that it had taken forty-six years to build the temple thus far (John 2:20 NIV). We know from secular history that Herod began to rebuild the temple around 20 BC. That makes the date of this first incident around AD 26 or 27, at the start of Jesus' earthly ministry.

As for the different days between Mark's account and Matthew's and Luke's, the most likely scenario is that Jesus cleansed the temple two days in a row. Remember, He'd done the exact same thing at a Passover three years earlier, and on that occasion He *first* braided a whip to drive them out. He obviously felt *very* strongly about what the merchants had been doing in the temple.

The other possibility is that Mark recorded the event out of order. "Mark. . .wrote down accurately whatsoever he remembered. It was not, however, in exact order that he related the sayings or deeds of Christ" (Eusebius, *Church History*, Book 3, Chapter 39:15)

51

Why do the Gospels give two different dates for the Passover supper?

๛

The Synoptic Gospels declare that Jesus and His disciples ate the Last Supper on Thursday after sundown, which was the Passover (Matthew 26:17–19; Mark 14:12–17; Luke 22:7–15). Indeed, Jewish Christians point out that it has the earmarks of being a Passover meal.

But John *seems* to say that this meal was "before the Feast of the Passover" and was an ordinary evening meal (John 13:1–2 NKJV). He also states that when the Jewish leaders took Jesus to Pilate the next morning, that "to avoid ceremonial uncleanness they did not enter the palace, because they wanted to be able to eat the Passover" (John 18:28 NIV). Later, John tells us this day "was the day of Preparation of the Passover" (John 19:14 NIV).

In his book *The New Testament Documents*, F. F. Bruce argued that a majority of Jews, including Jesus and His disciples, may have celebrated Passover a day before the chief priests and their circle. Perhaps different people followed different calendars—one pre-Exilic and one post-Exilic. Also, there may have been a practical reason: The priests may have simply been too exhausted from slaughtering thousands of lambs to observe Passover that day.

If, however, there was only *one* Passover meal, then when John says it was "just before the Passover Festival," he means the festival began with *that* meal. Even though the priests ate Passover that evening, they didn't want to be ritually defiled the next morning because there were a *series* of meals during the Passover Festival—the week-long Feast of Unleavened Bread. Also, "the day of Preparation" means Friday, the day before the Sabbath, so the "day of Preparation of the Passover" was the Friday during Passover week. This was also why that Saturday was "a special Sabbath" (John 19:14, 31 NIV).

52

Why do the four Gospels give conflicting accounts of Peter denying Jesus?

❧

At a casual glance, there appear to be contradictions between the Gospels regarding the details of Peter denying Jesus. But this is resolved if you look at all four Gospel accounts of this event side-by-side. Now, it should be pointed out that Matthew 26:57–75 and Mark 14:53–72 agree *very* closely. Not only do they tell the events in the same order, but their wording is almost identical.

Luke recounts the same details but in different order. Instead of describing Peter entering Caiaphas' courtyard, then the high priest interrogating Jesus, then refocusing on Peter, Luke tells Peter's story all together (Luke 22:54–62) *then* talks about Christ's appearance before Caiaphas (22:63–71). The events in the courtyard were happening at the same time as the events in Caiaphas's chamber, so it's valid to present them either way. Amazingly enough, despite Luke's different arrangement, his text is virtually identical.

John 18:12–27, however, adds new details. John tells us that the mob *first* took Jesus to Annas, Caiaphas's father-in-law. John knew this because he was there and was the one who got Peter into Annas's courtyard. John had firsthand information about Annas questioning Jesus, so *that's* what he writes about, while saying nothing about the interrogation at Caiaphas' house. Apparently, after Peter mingled with the servants in Annas' courtyard, he traveled with them when they took Jesus to Caiaphas's house.

When you read only Matthew, Mark, and Luke (which don't mention the stop at Annas's house), you might come to the conclusion that all three denials took place at Caiaphas's house. But John reveals that Peter first denied Jesus in Annas's courtyard then did so a second and third time in Caiaphas' courtyard. Another equally plausible interpretation, however, is that Peter denied Jesus *once* at Annas's house and then another *three* times at Caiaphas's house.

53

Were all Jews cursed for all time for crucifying Jesus?

❧

Not all Jewish people were brought under a curse for crucifying Christ, even though a mob in Pilate's courtyard cried out, "His blood be on us, and on our children" (Matthew 27:25 KJV).

Who, then, was responsible for crucifying Jesus? The Bible says "the chief priests, the scribes, and the elders of the people assembled at the palace of the high priest, who was called Caiaphas, and plotted to take Jesus by trickery and kill Him. But they said, 'Not during the feast, lest there be an uproar among the people'" (Matthew 26:3–5 NKJV).

Scripture also tells us that "They wanted to arrest him, but they were afraid of the crowds" (Matthew 21:46 NLT). The common Jewish people loved Jesus and "heard him gladly" (Mark 12:37 KJV). They were the "great multitude" who cheered when He rode into Jerusalem (John 12:12). Had the chief priests tried to arrest Jesus publicly, the people would have rioted. A multitude of such Jews became believers after Jesus rose from the dead (Acts 2:41; 4:4).

The Bible states that it was the small group of corrupt leaders—"the chief priests, the scribes, and the elders"—who plotted to kill Jesus (see Matthew 26:14, 47, 57, 59; 27:1–2; John 7:31–32). Jesus Himself had prophesied that He would die at the hands of the religious rulers (Matthew 16:21). These leaders sent a mob of zealous followers to arrest Jesus, and it was this crowd that filled Pilate's courtyard a few hours later, obeyed the rulers' orders, and called down a curse upon themselves (Matthew 26:47; 27:20, 24–25).

This curse was *not* brought upon the heads of *all* Jews, nor for *all time*. It was fulfilled in Jesus' enemies and their (then-grown) children forty years later in AD 70, when Roman legions besieged Jerusalem and slew those who had been fighting against them.

54

How should Christians respond to charges that the New Testament is anti-Semitic?

≈

Neither the Gospels nor the book of Acts nor the epistles of Paul are anti-Semitic. Sadly, however, it's true that some bigoted people down through the centuries have quoted them out of context to help incite hatred and pogroms against the Jewish people.

For example, Jesus said to certain Jews, "You are of your father the devil" (John 8:44 NKJV), but it's vital to remember that He was not speaking to *all* Jews, only to those who hated Him and were plotting to kill Him (8:37–40). Also, Jesus' scathing rebuke in Matthew 23 was directed at the hypocritical religious *leaders*, not the poor and vulnerable Jewish people those leaders were oppressing.

Six hundred years earlier, the prophet Jeremiah spoke out so sharply against the sins of his people that the rulers and priests denounced him as a false prophet, labeled him the enemy of the people, and threw him into prison (Jeremiah 28:5–11; 37:11–15; 38:1–4). Yet, within seventy years, the Jews realized that Jeremiah had been right and counted him among the greatest of their prophets. At times, Jesus' messages were so akin to Jeremiah's that many Jews thought He was Jeremiah come back to life (Matthew 16:13–14). Both Jeremiah and Jesus loved and wept over those who had rejected them (Lamentations 1:15–16; Luke 19:41– 44).

The book of Acts records how certain Jews persecuted Christians, and the apostle Paul had strong words for such men, but he talked about Gentile persecutors in the same breath (1 Thessalonians 2:14–16). Paul, who had great love for his fellow Jews, wrote, "I have great sorrow and continual grief in my heart" for them and "my heart's desire and prayer to God for Israel is that they may be saved" (Romans 9:2; 10:1 NKJV). Like Jeremiah and Jesus, Paul wept for his people.

55

How could the New Testament writers recite conversations they hadn't even heard?

We can easily understand how the apostles could have written about things they'd personally seen and heard. But the New Testament also quotes a number of private conversations between the ruling authorities and religious leaders.

For example, Matthew 14:1–12 tells us about King Herod Antipas's private dealings with and statements about John the Baptist, and Mark 6:14 relates Herod's musings about Jesus. How did the disciples learn these details? The answer can be found in scripture.

Luke 8:3 reports that Joanna (the wife of Chuza, King Herod's steward) was one of Jesus' close disciples. Luke also tells us that there was a prominent disciple in the early church named Manaen "who had been brought up with Herod the tetrarch" (Acts 13:1 NIV). Both of these people were likely excellent inside sources for the apostles.

But what about the following? Matthew 26:14–16 and 27:3–7 tell of Judas's private conversations with the chief priests; Matthew 28:2–4, 11–15 relates the conspiracy between the chief priests and the guards to deny Jesus' resurrection; Acts 4:13–17 specifically states that the religious leaders put the disciples out of the room before they held their council and did the same thing in Acts 5:29–39. So how were the gospel writers able to recount what their enemies had conspired to do when their plans were made behind closed doors?

Again, they had inside contacts. Both Nicodemus and Joseph of Arimathea were members of the Sanhedrin, the Jewish ruling council, yet were secret disciples of Jesus (Mark 15:43; John 3:1–2). Also, a number of lower-level priests who initially went along with the plots against Jesus became so upset with the cover-up and deception that they became Christians; in fact, "a great company of the priests were obedient to the faith" (Acts 6:7 KJV). Apparently, when they became believers, they passed along what they'd seen and heard.

56

How did Judas die—
by hanging himself or by
falling and bursting open?

&

At first read, there appears to be a contradiction between the accounts of Judas's death recorded in the Bible.

Matthew tells us that after Judas betrayed Jesus for thirty pieces of silver, "he threw down the pieces of silver in the temple and departed, and went and hanged himself. But the chief priests took the silver pieces and. . .bought with them the potter's field, to bury strangers in. Therefore that field has been called the Field of Blood to this day" (Matthew 27:5–8 NKJV).

Luke tells us, "With the payment he received for his wickedness, Judas bought a field; there he fell headlong, his body burst open and all his intestines spilled out. Everyone in Jerusalem heard about this, so they called that field in their language Akeldama, that is, Field of Blood" (Acts 1:18–19 NIV).

Luke doesn't contradict Matthew, however. Rather, he adds new details that give a fuller picture of Judas's death. The Potter's Field was located south of Jerusalem in the Valley of Hinnom and was known for its rich clay, which the locals used for making pottery. Judas hanged himself there. Apparently, his body wasn't discovered for a few days, and decomposition was well under way. When someone discovered the body and cut the rope, Judas' body hit the ground, burst, and his intestines spilled out.

With the potter's field now defiled, potters could no longer use its clay. No one would have bought their wares. The priests probably reminded the owners of this fact and then offered to buy the land with Judas's money. As far as Christians were concerned, it was called the Field of Blood because the money had been paid to betray Jesus' "innocent blood" (Matthew 27:4). However, the story of Judas's death and bloody fall was widely known in Jerusalem, and *they* considered it the Field of Blood for that reason.

57

Why does Matthew say Jeremiah gave a prophecy that Zechariah actually gave?

After Judas betrayed Jesus, he rushed back to the temple, threw down the thirty pieces of silver he'd received for his betrayal, and left. The priests then bought the potter's field with his money.

Matthew wrote that this event fulfilled a 550-year-old prophecy: "Then was fulfilled what was spoken by Jeremiah the prophet, saying, 'And they took the thirty pieces of silver, the value of Him who was priced, whom they of the children of Israel priced, and gave them for the potter's field, as the LORD directed me'" (Matthew 27:9–10 NKJV).

This is an amazingly fulfilled prophecy; however, Zechariah, not Jeremiah, was the one who delivered it: "So they weighed out for my wages thirty pieces of silver. And the LORD said to me, 'Throw it to the potter'—that princely price they set on me. So I took the thirty pieces of silver and threw them into the house of the LORD for the potter" (Zechariah 11:12–13 NKJV).

But these events *were* also foreshadowed in the book of Jeremiah. God told Jeremiah to take elders and priests into the same Valley of Hinnom (Tophet), hurl a potter's vessel on the ground, and prophesy, "Thus says the LORD of hosts: 'Even so I will break this people and this city, as one breaks a potter's vessel. . .and they shall bury them in Tophet' " (Jeremiah 19:11 NKJV).

Judas fell and broke open like the potter's vessel. And just as priests went to the valley with Jeremiah, six hundred years later priests went there to buy a field to "bury them in Tophet." Even Judas's lament, "I have betrayed innocent blood" (Matthew 27:4 NIV) is seen in Jeremiah's declaration that they were guilty of "the blood of the innocent" (Jeremiah 19:4 NIV).

Matthew was referring to prophetic imagery in the books of Jeremiah *and* Zechariah and, as was sometimes done, cited only the *major* prophet (compare Mark 1:2–3 with Isaiah 40:3 and Malachi 3:1).

58

What did the writing above
Jesus' cross actually say?

~

In Roman times, when a criminal was sentenced to be crucified, it was customary to write the charges against him on a small board, called in Latin a *titulus*. Someone carried this board in front of the condemned man as he bore his cross to the place of execution. One of the man's executioners then nailed the board to the cross above the crucified man's head.

Matthew tells us that the charge affixed to the top of Jesus' cross read, "This is Jesus the King of the Jews" (Matthew 27:37 NLT). Mark tells us that it read simply, "The King of the Jews" (Mark 15:26 NLT). Luke tells us that the writing said, "This is the King of the Jews" (Luke 23:38 NLT). And finally, John tells us that the writing said, "Jesus of Nazareth, the King of the Jews" (John 19:19 NLT).

While the meaning of all four phrases is the same, why are there differences? The answer is found in John 19:20 (NKJV), which states that "it was written in Hebrew, Greek, and Latin." The wording in each of these three languages was slightly different.

In Latin, John's title reads *Iesus Nazarenus Rex Iudaeorum*, and from an early date Latin Christians used the initials *INRI* as a symbol of Christ. Now, John's text is the only one that mentions Nazareth (hence the "N"), plus he's the only one who refers to the charge as a "title" (Latin *titulus*), so John quoted the Latin reading.

Matthew (writing for the Jews) quoted the Hebrew wording and Luke (writing for the Greeks) quoted the Greek wording. In all cases, the core of the accusation was, "The King of the Jews," so Mark (known for his brief style) simply stated that. Jesus' enemies wanted this accusation changed to read, "He said, 'I am the King of the Jews,'" but Pilate refused (John 19:21–22 NKJV).

59

Why do the Gospel writers often relate the same incident differently?

Although Matthew, Mark, and Luke all drew their stories about Jesus from a common source, each one was inspired to select stories and edit them according to the needs of their audiences. Matthew wrote to convince the Jews that Jesus was the Messiah. Luke, writing for the Greeks, was often led to choose different stories, and even when he related the *same* events, he frequently related different aspects of them.

For example, in the final moments before Jesus died on the cross, Matthew records Him saying, "My God, my God, why have you forsaken me?" (Matthew 27:46 NIV). Later, Matthew tells us Jesus cried out with a loud voice and died—but doesn't tell us His final words (verse 50). Luke, for his part, *doesn't* record Jesus asking why God had forsaken Him. Instead he tells us, "Jesus called out with a loud voice, 'Father, into your hands I commit my spirit.'

When he had said this, he breathed his last" (Luke 23:46 NIV).

Matthew chose the saying he did because it was a direct quote from Psalm 22:1. In Psalm 22 David prophesied with chilling accuracy about the crucifixion of Israel's Messiah (see verses 14–18). Luke's Greek audience didn't have a background in the Jewish scriptures, so this quote would have meant nothing to them—and would have just confused them. They did, however, have a strong philosophical belief that a god (or divine man) would act calmly in the face of tragedy. Luke selected his quote with that in mind.

Jesus *did* utter both declarations, and since Luke was writing a new Gospel—and not simply copying Matthew's Gospel word for word—he chose different details to reach his readers. Christians believe this was not simply an editorial decision but that God inspired him in this.

60

How do we know Jesus actually died on the cross? Isn't it possible He just fell unconscious and later revived in the cool tomb?

People who don't want to believe that Jesus rose from the dead have come up with several theories stating that He never died in the first place and that He may have just *appeared* to resurrect. One of the most persistent (but pathetic) hypotheses is the Swoon Theory, which holds that Jesus just fainted from pain and exhaustion and only *appeared* dead. Roman soldiers then allowed Him to be taken down from the cross and placed in the tomb, where He revived. A variation of this theory states that the vinegar Jesus sipped (John 19:28–30) was actually a drug that induced a temporary comatose state.

However, falling unconscious would have caused Jesus to die within minutes. A well-known aspect of crucifixion is that the victim had to continually push himself up with his legs in order to breathe.

Remaining hanging in a slumped position caused quick asphyxiation.

In addition, to make *sure* Jesus was dead, a Roman soldier pierced His side with a spear, impaling His heart, and causing blood to gush out (John 19:31–37).

Other conspiracy theorists doubt that Jesus died after hanging on the cross for only six hours, since it normally took two to four days for the victim of crucifixion to die. Pilate himself was surprised that Jesus expired so quickly (Mark 15:44). Medical authorities, however, point out that when Jesus was whipped with a flagellum, the many deep cuts caused considerable blood loss and induced hypovolemic shock. Jesus had been so weakened by the ordeal that He was unable to carry His crossbar to Golgotha (Matthew 27:26, 32).

Even skeptics admit that *had* Jesus somehow (barely) survived His crucifixion, He'd have been so weakened and pitiful that He could hardly have presented Himself as the Lord of Life.

There can be no doubt that Jesus was dead when He was taken down from the cross—or that God raised Him from the dead three days later.

61

How do we know Jesus' disciples didn't steal His body from the tomb and falsely claim He had been raised from the dead?

❧

Another argument against Jesus' literal resurrection is the theory that His disciples stole His body from the tomb so that they could claim that He had been raised from the dead in fulfillment of Old Testament prophecies about the Messiah. After all, skeptics point out, Jesus *had* repeatedly told His disciples He'd be killed and then rise again (Matthew 16:21; 17:22–23; 20:17–19). Even Jesus' enemies were aware of this prophecy (Matthew 27:62–63).

However, *because* the chief priests were worried that someone could steal the body, they assigned several soldiers (whether Roman soldiers or Jewish Temple guards) to stand watch at Jesus' tomb. When this failed to stop Jesus from rising, the priests went into "damage control" mode and started a rumor that Jesus' disciples had stolen His body (Matthew 27:62–66; 28:1–4, 11–15).

Also, even though Jesus had repeatedly talked about it, the disciples didn't know "what the rising from the dead meant" (Mark 9:9–10 NKJV). Plus "they did not know the Scripture, that He must rise again from the dead" (John 20:9 NKJV). Only later did Jesus explain *which* Old Testament scriptures His resurrection had fulfilled (Luke 24:27; Acts 2:24–31).

Plus, the mob that arrested Jesus had so terrified His disciples that they scattered into the night. Even after news of His resurrection reached them, they remained huddled in a house with the door locked, for fear of their enemies (Mark 14:43, 50; John 20:19).

Very importantly, stealing Jesus' body then publicly proclaiming what they *knew* to be a *lie* would have gone against everything Jesus stood for and had taught the disciples. It also contradicts the proclamations in the book of Acts that the disciples believed Jesus *had* resurrected and were willing to suffer martyrdom for that belief.

Finally, such a scenario doesn't explain how the disciples saw Jesus after His resurrection (1 Corinthians 15:3–8).

62

Weren't Jesus' disciples
suffering hallucinations
when they "saw" Him again?

୶

Some have held that it is possible that the disciples
experienced emotion-induced hallucinations when
they saw Jesus after His death. However, while
individuals may hallucinate, a crowd doesn't see such
shared visions. But that's exactly what the *disciples*
themselves thought at first.

When the women who followed Jesus reported
that they'd seen Him, the men thought they'd been
seeing things and "they did not believe the women,
because their words seemed to them like nonsense"
(Luke 24:11 NIV).

The disciples' opinion about what the women
had really seen changed immediately when Jesus
entered the room and ten of *them* saw Him. They
knew they were not having hallucinations but "were
startled and frightened, thinking they saw a ghost"
(Luke 24:37 NIV).

Jesus immediately set them straight. He said, "Why are your hearts filled with doubt? Look at my hands. Look at my feet. You can see that it's really me. Touch me and make sure that I am not a ghost, because ghosts don't have bodies, as you see that I do" (Luke 24:38–39 NLT). He commanded them to touch Him and they surely did. Within *one* minute, Jesus was upgraded in their minds from a hallucination to a ghost to solid reality.

To further prove He was really alive, Jesus asked for some food. "So they gave Him a piece of a broiled fish and some honeycomb. And He took it and ate in their presence" (Luke 24:42–43 NKJV). The disciples also ate and drank *with* Jesus on other occasions (Acts 10:39–41).

Thomas wasn't there that first time Jesus appeared to the other ten remaining disciples. Seeing Jesus and even touching Him wasn't enough to convince him. He insisted He'd have to stick his finger in Jesus' wounds before he'd believe. And Jesus gave him that opportunity (John 20:24–28).

Yes, Jesus really rose from the dead, and He "presented Himself alive after His suffering by many infallible proofs" (Acts 1:3 NKJV).

63

How can apparent contradictions in the Gospel accounts of what happened that first Easter Sunday morning be explained?

People are often baffled by the differences in the four Gospels' details of the events surrounding Jesus' resurrection. Each gospel recounts different combinations of women coming to His tomb and vary as to what they saw and heard. Some assume that the Gospels contradict one another so much that each invalidates the others' testimony.

This is evidence, however, that the Gospel writers are truthful, since witnesses who conspire to lie are very careful to make their stories line up—even in the tiniest details. In a court of law, superficial differences between testimonies actually render witnesses more credible.

Also, the differing Gospel reports of this event *can* be harmonized. All four accounts have been contracted into brief narratives, with all the women named together—yet there were almost certainly two groups of women who set out that morning from separate locations at different times. Mary Magdalene led one of those groups (John 20:1), and Susana, Salome, or Joanna—all prominent female disciples—led the other (Luke 8:1–3; 24:10; Mark 16:1).

It also helps clarify the order of events if you bear in mind that Mary Magdalene told Peter and John the news first, then *later* told the main group of apostles. John owned a house nearby, in Jerusalem, and he and Peter were there that morning (John 18:15–16; 19:26–27; 20:1–3). The other disciples, except for Thomas, had apparently retreated to Bethany, two miles distant, where they had previously stayed (Matthew 21:17; 26:56; John 20:24). So Mary and the women reported to two different groups in succession.

Also, the tomb was near the city (John 19:20, 41), so it didn't take long to travel there and back. Mary Magdalene is known to have visited the tomb twice (John 20:1–11) and probably went back a third time with the other Mary (Matthew 28:9–10).

64

Why do Stephen's statements about Abraham contradict what Genesis says?

જી

In the New Testament, Stephen said, "The God of glory appeared to our father Abraham [Abram] when he was in Mesopotamia, before he dwelt in Haran, and said to him, 'Get out of your country and from your relatives, and come to a land that I will show you.' Then he came out of the land of the Chaldeans and dwelt in Haran. And from there, when his father was dead, He moved him to this land" (Acts 7:2–4 NKJV).

Yet Genesis 11:31 seems to say that *first* Abraham's father Terah took his family, including Abraham, from Ur of the Chaldeans to Haran. *Then* Genesis 12:1–5 says that God called Abraham from Haran into Canaan. So which account is right?

Genesis 12:1 *doesn't* say, "Then the LORD said to Abram: 'Get out of your country. . . .'" Rather, it says, "Now the LORD had said to Abram: 'Get out of your country. . . .'" (Genesis 12:1–2 NKJV). In other words, God had *already* spoken to Abraham back in Ur.

But this still leaves another question: Genesis

11:26 (NKJV) says, "Terah lived seventy years, and begot Abram, Nahor, and Haran." Then verse 32 says that Terah died in Haran at 205 years of age. But both Genesis and Acts say that Abraham left Haran *after* his father died. Yet Genesis 12:4 says that Abraham was seventy-five years old when he left Haran, and 70 + 75 = 145, not 205. Did Terah live another sixty years after Abraham left Haran?

No. The answer is that Abram, Nahor, and Haran weren't triplets but were born in separate years. One son was born when their father was seventy, another some years after, and Abraham was born sixty years after the firstborn son—quite possibly from a second wife. Abraham was mentioned first simply because he was the most notable son.

65

**Why did Stephen say
seventy-five of Jacob's descendants
went to Egypt when only seventy did?**

ঞ

Stephen said, "Joseph sent for his father Jacob and his
whole family, seventy-five in all" (Acts 7:14 NIV). Yet
Genesis says, "With the two sons who had been born
to Joseph in Egypt, the members of Jacob's family,
which went to Egypt, were seventy in all" (Genesis
46:27 NIV).

How did Stephen come up with seventy-five?
Well, since he was a Hellenistic Jew (one who spoke
and read Greek, not Hebrew), he quoted from
the Greek translation of the Old Testament, the
Septuagint. In this translation, Genesis 46:27 says:
"And the sons of Joseph, who were born to him in
the land of Egypt, were nine souls; all the souls of the
house of Jacob who came with Joseph into Egypt,
were seventy-five souls" (translated by Sir L. C. L.
Brenton, 1851).

In this instance, the Septuagint gives a fuller

number than the Masoretic text, listing nine sons of Joseph, not just his first two. Joseph was the *last* of his brothers to get married, and he had only two sons when Jacob came to Egypt (Genesis 48:5–6)—but Joseph had seven more sons after that.

When you subtract Er and Onan, who died in Canaan, and Ephraim and Manasseh, who were born in Egypt, you have this equation: 70 − 4 = 66. That's why Genesis 46:26 (NKJV) specifies: "All the persons who went with Jacob to Egypt. . .were sixty-six persons in all." Thus, 66 + Joseph's 9 = 75.

Note: these seventy-five people were Jacob's sons and grandsons—not his daughters and granddaughters. At that time, women weren't named in genealogical lists. Dinah was an exception (Genesis 46:15). But Jacob's sons had wives, and Jacob likely had as many daughters as sons (These unnamed daughters are mentioned in Genesis 37:34–35.). So the *total* number of Jacob's family who came down into Egypt was probably close to 150.

66

Who bought the field in Shechem— Jacob or Abraham?

෫

Stephen said, "Jacob went down to Egypt and there he and our fathers died. From there they were removed to Shechem and laid in the tomb which Abraham had purchased for a sum of money from the sons of Hamor in Shechem" (Acts 7:15–16 NASB).

When Jacob returned to Canaan, *he* bought a field from "the sons of Hamor" (Amorites) in Shechem (Genesis 33:18–20). Abraham, however, had purchased a field with a cave-tomb from "the sons of Heth" (Hittites) at Hebron (Genesis 23). He was buried there, as were Isaac and Jacob (Genesis 25:7–10; 49:29–33; 50:12–13).

Joseph was entombed at Shechem (Joshua 24:32), and it appears from Acts 7 that his brothers were also. But the question is: If Abraham bought land in Hebron but *not* in Shechem, did Stephen get his facts mixed up?

Bible commentators point out that it was

common practice for Jews to contract long, complex narratives into brief statements, so they'd have understood Stephen doing that—even if it seems odd to us today.

However, consider that 205 years before Jacob bought a field and erected an altar by "the" terebinth tree of Shechem (Genesis 33:18–20; 35:4), Abraham entered Canaan and stopped at Shechem, where he *also* built an altar by "the" famous terebinth tree (Genesis 12:5–7). Now, did Abraham build his altar then abandon it? The spot was sacred to him. God had appeared there and promised, "To your descendants I will give this land" (Genesis 12:7 NKJV). Abraham likely bought the field with the nearby hillside to ensure that his altar remained standing after he moved.

But after a 205-year absence, the Amorites likely reclaimed the land. So Jacob, desiring to reconfirm the promise made to *him* (Abraham's "descendant"), was constrained to buy it again. Then he rebuilt the altar.

67

What exactly did the men traveling to Damascus with Saul (Paul) hear. . .or *not* hear?

☙

Around AD 35, Paul (then called Saul) was traveling to Damascus to persecute Christians. One account says, "As he journeyed. . .suddenly a light shone around him from heaven. Then he fell to the ground, and heard a voice saying to him, 'Saul, Saul, why are you persecuting Me?'" (Acts 9:3–4 NKJV). This was Jesus speaking. Verse 7 adds, "And the men who journeyed with him stood speechless, hearing a voice but seeing no one."

Yet when Paul spoke to a crowd in Jerusalem some twenty years later, he said, "And those who were with me indeed saw the light and were afraid, but they did not hear the voice of Him who spoke to me" (Acts 22:9 NKJV).

First we are told that Paul's companions heard a voice, but then Paul says they didn't hear a voice. Which one is correct?

They both are. The Greek word *phone*, translated as "voice," means both "voice" and "sound." Thus the New International Version says: "The men traveling with Saul. . .heard the sound but did not see anyone" (Acts 9:7 NIV), and has Paul stating that his fellow travelers "did not understand the voice of him who was speaking to me" (Acts 22:9 NIV).

Paul saw and heard Jesus (1 Corinthians 15:8), but his companions weren't spiritually attuned. They saw the light but couldn't make out Jesus' form; they heard a sound but couldn't understand the words— and possibly weren't even sure it was a voice.

A similar thing had happened before in scripture. Jesus prayed, " 'Father, glorify Your name.' Then a voice came out of heaven: 'I have both glorified it, and will glorify it again.' So the crowd of people who stood by and heard it were saying that it had thundered; others were saying, 'An angel has spoken to Him' " (John 12:28–29 NASB; see also Daniel 10:7).

68

Why weren't Paul's pastoral epistles part of the first Bible canon?

Paul wrote ten of his thirteen epistles between AD 51 and his release from house arrest in Rome in AD 62. After that, he wrote his final letters, called pastoral epistles. They were 1 Timothy and Titus (written AD 63–65) and 2 Timothy (written during his final Roman imprisonment in around AD 67–68).

When the heretic Marcion compiled his canon in AD 144, he included Paul's first ten epistles, but not the final three. This has led some critics to question whether the pastoral epistles even existed by then— or if someone else (using Paul's name) wrote them later on.

Also, these three letters contain words and phrases Paul never used in his other epistles. For example, the expression "a trustworthy saying" appears five times in the pastoral epistles, but nowhere else in Paul's epistles. The words *godly* and *godliness* appear ten times in these epistles, but nowhere in Paul's letters. Based on these and other stylistic differences, many skeptics believe these epistles were later forgeries written in Paul's name.

However, the overall evidence is strong that Paul indeed wrote these epistles. The differences in vocabulary and word usage can be sufficiently explained by (a) Paul's recent experiences (he had been to Spain and back), (b) his immersion in the Latin West, and (c) the passage of several years. The early church never doubted that Paul had written these three epistles. In fact, in the AD 170 Muratorian Fragment, an official church list of Bible books, all three are mentioned as part of the New Testament canon.

As for why Marcion included only Paul's ten early epistles, it's likely that these epistles were compiled into one scroll for posterity during Paul's first imprisonment in AD 61–62, when it wasn't certain he'd be released. They would have circulated as one unit before the later three epistles were added. Marcion likely had access to the earlier compilation.

69

Did Paul and James disagree on the roles of grace and works for salvation?

❧

The apostle Paul taught: "For it is by grace you have been saved, through faith—and this is not from yourselves, it is the gift of God—not by works" (Ephesians 2:8–9 NIV). However, many people assume that the apostle James's basic message is summed up by *this* verse: "You see then that a man is justified by works, and not by faith only" (James 2:24 NKJV).

It is simplistic to pit these verses against each other as if they represent conflicting views. Paul held that we're saved by grace and not by works, but he agreed with James's position (James 2:14–17) that mere mental assent to faith in Jesus won't save a person whose actions shout the opposite. Paul also warned against those who *professed* to know God "but in works they deny Him" (Titus 1:16 NKJV).

Doing good works won't save you, but Jesus taught that the fruit your life bears is the surest proof of who you really are (Matthew 7:20). This is why Paul stressed that "those who have believed in God should be careful to maintain good works" (Titus 3:8 NKJV)—not to keep yourself saved, but because God inspires you to do good works.

So did Paul and James believe the same thing? Yes, and this issue was settled back in AD 50. Some Christian Pharisees had argued that Jews and Gentiles alike had to obey the Law of Moses to be saved (Acts 15:1, 5). However, in a meeting under the leadership of Peter *and* James, Peter summed up the Jerusalem church's position when he stated, "We believe that we are all saved the same way, by the undeserved grace of the Lord Jesus" (Acts 15:11 NLT). Notice the "we."

This was James' position as well—that both Jews and Gentiles were saved not by good works but by *undeserved grace.*

70

Why are the words sometimes different when New Testament writers quote Old Testament passages?

The writers of the New Testament frequently quoted the Jewish scriptures (the Old Testament) to show how they were fulfilled in Christ. The wording of the quoted passages is often exactly the same as what we read in the present-day Old Testament, which is based upon the Masoretic Text. However, there are sometimes differences. For example, notice the variation between Psalm 40:6 and Hebrews 10:5.

Why the differences? Well, in the centuries before Christ, millions of Jews throughout the Greek-speaking world no longer spoke or read Hebrew, so in 285–250 BC Jewish scholars began translating the Hebrew scriptures into Greek. This translation, called the Septuagint—Latin for *seventy* (seventy translators, though one legend holds that there were seventy-two)—was completed in 132 BC. For centuries, this was most Jewish people's official version of the scriptures.

Paul and other New Testament writers often quoted from this Greek translation.

So when there are differences between the Masoretic Text and the Septuagint, which is right? Many Christians believe that since the Septuagint was translated 285–132 BC, it was based on an earlier and more accurate Hebrew reading than the later Masoretic Text. They give a number of examples to support this view.

Here's one: Psalm 22 prophetically describes Jesus' crucifixion. In the Septuagint, verse 16 says "They have pierced my hands and feet." But in the present-day Masoretic text, the same verse reads, "Like a lion are my hands and feet." Which reading is correct? Is the Hebrew word *k'aru* (pierced) the original reading, or is *k'ari* (like a lion)? In the two thousand-year-old *Psalms Scroll*, written in Hebrew and found at Nahal Hever, Psalm 22:16 agrees with the Septuagint.

The Septuagint isn't *always* more accurate than the Masoretic Text (since not all of its books were translated with the same precision) but in many places it is.

71

When did Christians realize that the letters of the New Testament were also scripture?

Christians recognized most books of the New Testament as scripture very early on. This was because Jesus was the Messiah, the Son of God who had resurrected from the dead, who fulfilled the Old Testament scriptures and ushered in a new era. Therefore, the story and words of Jesus—and the written versions of the Gospels—were accepted as equal to the Old Testament scriptures.

In AD 63–65, Paul put the written sayings of Jesus on the same level as the Law of Moses. He wrote, "For the Scripture says, 'You shall not muzzle an ox while it treads out the grain,' and 'The laborer is worthy of his wages'" (1 Timothy 5:18 NKJV). The first passage Paul quoted was Deuteronomy 25:4, and the second passage was Luke 10:7.

In addition, early Christians recognized that the Holy Spirit had inspired the apostles. Paul wrote, "If anyone thinks himself to be a prophet or spiritual, let him acknowledge that the things which I write to you are the commandments of the Lord" (1 Corinthians 14:37 NKJV).

The apostle Peter acknowledged this very thing. As mentioned in a previous Q&A, most of Paul's letters had been circulating together since about AD 62. We know Peter had studied them, because he wrote in AD 65–68, "This is what our beloved brother Paul also wrote to you with the wisdom God gave him—speaking of all these things in all of his letters. . . . And those who are ignorant and unstable have twisted his letters to mean something quite different, just as they do with other parts of Scripture" (2 Peter 3:15–16 NLT).

It took longer for other books—Revelation, for example—to be accepted, but the church acknowledged the bulk of the New Testament as canonical and as Scripture by AD 68.

72

Why did it take Christians over three hundred years to agree on which books belonged in the New Testament?

The Synoptic Gospels (Matthew, Mark, and Luke) were acknowledged as Scripture in AD 63–65, and Paul's first ten epistles were accepted by AD 68. John completed his gospel around AD 90, and it was almost immediately accepted as canonical. Soon, the church accepted 1 and 2 Timothy, Titus, Hebrews, 1 John, and 1 Peter.

In his writings, the church father Irenaeus (AD 130–200) quoted from twenty-three of our twenty-seven New Testament books, and the Muratorian list shows that the church in Rome accepted the book of Revelation before AD 170. Virtually all the current New Testament books had been accepted by that date. But why weren't *all* Christians in agreement until AD 367?

In *Ecclesiastical History*, written in AD 300, Eusebius listed the "Recognized Books," then said,

"Those that are disputed, yet familiar to most, include the epistles known as James, Jude, and 2 Peter, and those called 2 and 3 John." As for Revelation, he wrote that "some reject it, others include it among the Recognized Books" (Eusebius, *Ecclesiastical History*, Book 3, Chapter 25).

One of the reasons for slow universal acceptance of all these books was that the apostles Paul, Peter, and John were no longer around to pass judgment on them. Plus, communication was slow and more difficult back then, and epistles like James—written in Judea for Jewish Christians—weren't widely known in the church at large. The church fathers also exercised great caution before officially accepting an epistle as scripture.

In AD 367, Athanasius, Bishop of Alexandria, listed the same New Testament books we have today. However, he was not making a *decision* as to which books were scripture but merely reminding his readers what the church had already acknowledged.

73

Did Constantine and the Roman Empire *doctor* the New Testament manuscripts?

Some Bible critics argue that after Constantine accepted Christianity, the Roman Empire took control of the Bible and then "doctored" it. In other words, there was a deliberate conspiracy to change the Bible text. The Romans' motive, the detractors say, was to better control the people.

However, there's absolutely no evidence that the Roman Empire changed the scriptures. In fact, when they are asked *which* parts of the text the Romans changed, most critics are at a loss for words. A logical assumption is that the Romans would have *added* passages like Romans 13:1–7, which commands Christians to be subject to the government, to not resist those in authority, to pay taxes, and to consider the authorities "God's ministers." Presumably, they would *also* have added 1 Peter 2:13–17 (or beefed it up if it existed), which admonishes Christians to submit to *every* law of man, and to "honor the king [Caesar]."

The problem with this theory, however, is that the Bible as we have it today can be checked against *earlier* copies of the scriptures. Constantine became a Christian in AD 312 and in AD 331 ordered Eusebius to provide fifty Bibles for churches. However, copies of the scriptures exist from *before* these dates. The Beatty Papyrus P46 contains Romans 13, which is identical to the text we have today. Scholars date it to AD 175–225— *at least* eighty years before Constantine became a Christian. As for Peter's commands, the Bodmer Papyrus P72 contains the entire book of 1 Peter—including the passage 2:13–17. This document dates to AD 200, some 112 years before Constantine's conversion.

The full collections of the Beatty and the Bodmer papyri contain the majority of the New Testament, and *no* changes that can be construed as "Roman" are evident between these and post-Constantine copies. The conclusion: The Romans didn't entertain such motives and didn't take such actions.

74

Why does the epistle of Jude quote from the non-biblical book of Enoch?

❧

Jude 14–15 (NKJV) says, "Now Enoch, the seventh from Adam, prophesied about these men also, saying, 'Behold, the Lord comes with ten thousands of His saints, to execute judgment on all, to convict all who are ungodly among them of all their ungodly deeds which they have committed in an ungodly way, and of all the harsh things which ungodly sinners have spoken against Him.'"

This prophecy isn't from the Old Testament but from the non-biblical Book 1 of Enoch, which—though purportedly written by the Enoch of Genesis 5:24—didn't exist until about two centuries before Christ. So why did Jude quote from it as if it were inspired by God? Well, just because he quoted a sentence from it doesn't mean he considered the *entire* book inspired. He was simply quoting a well-known statement that proved his point.

The apostle Paul often quoted Greek authors

for the same reason. For example, Paul wrote, "One of them, a prophet of their own, said, 'Cretans are always liars, evil beasts, lazy gluttons.' This testimony is true" (Titus 1:12–13 NKJV). Paul was quoting *Cretica* by Epimenides (500s BC), a Cretan poet said to have made several true predictions. Does this mean Paul endorsed everything Epimenides said? By no means! In *Cretica*, Epimenides wrote of Zeus, "thou livest and abidest forever." Of course, Paul wouldn't have agreed with that statement—or used it in one of his letters.

Acts 17:28 also records Paul quoting Epimenides and also citing the Cilician poet Aratus (315–240 BC). In 1 Corinthians 15:33, he quoted the play *Thais* by the Greek playwright Menander (342–291 BC). *Thais* was a comedy about a prostitute—so Paul obviously would not have considered it God-inspired. It's unlikely he even watched the play. The quote he repeated was a common proverb among Greeks of his day.

75

Why were the Gnostic "gospels" excluded from the New Testament?

What most people know about Gnosticism is what they learn from reading the book *The Da Vinci Code* or from watching TV documentaries on the subject. The impression these works give is that Gnostics were simply spiritually minded Christians seeking to know God (the Greek word *gnōsis* means "knowledge"), enjoy religious freedom, and worship "the divine feminine." When you sit down to study their writings, however, you're in for some very bizarre reading.

Gnostics wrote the "gospels" of Thomas, Philip, Judas, Mary, etc., and some recent works insist that the early church wrongfully excluded the "truths" of the Gnostic gospels from the New Testament. Such TV shows and books leave the impression that the Gnostic gospels show us what the "real" and "very human" Jesus was like.

The opposite is true, however. The historical

Gospels—Matthew, Mark, Luke, and John—describe Jesus as real and very human. They speak of Him being hungry, thirsty, tired, and angry. The Gnostic gospels, on the other hand, describe Him as a disembodied spirit who only *appeared* to have a body. Instead of healing the sick and feeding the hungry, the Gnostic "Jesus" rambles on and on in long, esoteric philosophical discourses.

The Gospel of Thomas is merely a collection of sayings Jesus supposedly said, whereas the Secret Book According to John contains intellectual speculation on endless spiritual realms and ages and so-called manifestations of God. It distorts Jesus' simple Gospel into something unspeakably complex.

Gnostics were *not*, as some claim, the first Christians. They appeared some sixty years after Christ, and it wasn't before AD 130 that they had fully developed their theology. Gnostics wrote their spurious "gospels" in the second century AD, fraudulently claiming that Thomas, Mary Magdalene, and Judas had written them earlier.

The leaders of the early church easily recognized these writings as non-historical frauds, and therefore excluded them from the New Testament canon.

One final question:
What will I do about Jesus?

&

If you're a Christian, I trust that these Q&As have
strengthened your faith, "so you can be certain of the
truth of everything you were taught" (Luke 1:4 NLT).

Yes, Christianity is solidly rooted in real time. It
is a historical faith, one that has time and again been
validated by archaeological discoveries. The writers of
the New Testament were eyewitnesses of the events
they describe. As the apostle Peter wrote, "We have
not followed cunningly devised fables, when we made
known unto you the power and coming of our Lord
Jesus Christ, but were eyewitnesses" (2 Peter 1:16 KJV).

If you're not yet a Christian, then here's a
question you might want to ponder: "What then
shall I do with Jesus who is called Christ?" (Matthew
27:22 NKJV). As you have seen, there are answers to
questions people have about the Bible. I hope that
you've seen that trusting in Jesus Christ doesn't mean
shutting off your mind and ignoring reason. It's not
a leap in the dark. Christianity is understandable and

makes sense. The apostle Paul declared that it is "true and reasonable" (Acts 26:25 NIV).

The four Gospels are historical accounts of the life of Jesus. They also testify that He has power to perform miracles. But more than anything, they were "written that you may believe that Jesus is the Christ, the Son of God, and that believing you may have life in His name" (John 20:31 NKJV). How do you do this? "If you confess with your mouth that Jesus is Lord and believe in your heart that God raised him from the dead, you will be saved. For it is by believing in your heart that you are made right with God, and it is by confessing with your mouth that you are saved" (Romans 10:9–10 NLT).